On Research Guide, delete asset if weeded

200.9 M848
Morgan, John H. (John Henry), 1945-
"In the beginning-- " : the Paleolithic origins of religious consciousness
66363

"In The Beginning…"

...books by John H. Morgan...

Studies in Ecclesiastical Sociology
The Diaconate Today: A Study of Clergy Attitudes
Who Become Bishop?: A Study of Episcopal Priests
Women Priests: A Study of an Emerging Ministry
Wives of Priests: A Study of Episcopal Clergy Spouses
  (with Linda B. Morgan)
Scholar, Priest, and Pastor: Ministry Priorities Among Clergy Today

Religion and the Social Sciences
In the Absence of God: Religious Humanism as Spiritual Journey
Naturally Good: A Behavioral History of Moral Development
In Search of Meaning: From Freud to Teilhard de Chardin
The Anglican Mind: A Theological Compendium
  (17th Century English Thought)
Catholic Spirituality: A Guide for Protestants
Understanding Religion and Culture: Essays in Honor of Clifford Geertz
Sociological Thought from Comte to Sorokin (with M. F. Abraham)
From Freud to Frankl: Our Modern Search for Personal Meaning
The United Inheritance: The Shaker Adventure in Communal Life
Interfacing Geertz and Tillich: A Convergence of Meaning
Being Human: Perspectives on Meaning and Interpretation

Research Tools and Methodologies
From Beginning to End: Internet Research and the Writing Process
  (with Russell Neitzke)
Library Research in Sociology
Library Research in Psychology
Sociopharmacology: A Research Bibliography
Genetics and Behavior: A Research Bibliography
Sociobiology: A Research Bibliography

Poetry Anthologies and Celebrations
Celebrating T.S. Eliot: Contemporary Poetry on the Eliot Centennial
Newman of Oxford: A Centennial Celebration in Poetry
Frost in Spring: An Anthology in Memoriam to Robert Frost
Emily Dickinson: A First Book Affair (1890-1990)
  Emerson of Harvard: A Celebrative Bicentennial (1803-1882)

"In The Beginning..."

The Paleolithic Origins of Religious Consciousness

John H. Morgan

Cloverdale Books
South Bend

"In The Beginning..." The Paleolithic Origins of Religious Consciousness

John H. Morgan

Copyright © 2007 by John H. Morgan
ALL RIGHTS RESERVED

Published by
Cloverdale Books
An Imprint of Cloverdale Corporation
South Bend, Indiana 46601
www.CloverdaleBooks.com

Library of Congress Cataloging-in-Publication Data

Morgan, John H. (John Henry), 1945-
  "In the beginning-- " : the Paleolithic origins of religious consciousness / John H. Morgan.
     p. cm.
  Summary: "This study explores the origins of religious consciousness by means of a systematic analysis of the ritualized burial of the dead and cave art as evidenced in Paleolithic remains. It is suggested here that religion is a natural manifestation of emerging human consciousness demonstrated by empirical archeological artifacts as an integral component to cultural evolution"--Provided by publisher.
  Includes bibliographical references and index.
  ISBN-13: 978-1-929569-41-0 (pbk.)
  ISBN-10: 1-929569-41-6 (pbk.)
  1. Religion, Prehistoric. 2. Paleolithic period. 3. Antiquities, Prehistoric. I. Title.

GN799.R4M67 2007
200.9'012--dc22

                              2007039771

Book Design by Gregory Koehler

Printed in the United States of America
on recycled paper made from 100% post-consumer waste

With enduring gratitude to the institutions in my life

--

The Hartford Seminary Foundation
Harvard, Yale, and Princeton
The University of Oxford

Where I began, where I learned, where I taught.

Thanks for the privilege.

Table of Contents

Acknowledgements   *xi*

Introduction   1

CHAPTER ONE
Psycho-Social Expressiveness
Ingredients of Humanness)   13

    Aesthetic Expressiveness   14
    Survival Wisdom   16
    Community Development   17
    Speculation (Religion in the Making)   18

CHAPTER TWO
Tripartite Matrix of Evolution
(Biological capacity, Sociological opportunity, Psychological inclination)   21

    Biogenesis - Bipedalism / Stereoscopic Vision / Verbal
        Acuity / Opposable Digitation   22
    Sociogenesis - Social Interaction / Linguistic Acuity /
        Socio-dynamic Connectedness   26
    Psychogenesis - Reflective Self-awareness / Reflexive
        Cognition / Psychodynamic Expressiveness   29

Chapter Three
Hominidal Sequencing
(Aptitude Development)   33

The Branching: Survival based on ever-increasing Skills
    Aptitude   33
Neanderthal   34
Cro-Magnon   37
Ideology and Behavior
    (The Vortex of Thought and Action)   41
Memory and Imagination (Storytelling as Survival
    Conveyance)   43
Fundamentally Human Propensities   44

Chapter Four
Religion How a Community Handles Awe, Wonder, and Reverence   45

Herbert Spencer's Unknown and Unknowable   45
The Unknown (The triumph of scientific inquiry)   46
The Unknowable (The triumph of religious
    explanation)   47
Religion and Its Function   51
Burial Of The Dead – A Classic Demonstration   56

Chapter Five
Culture: How a Community Lives in the World   67

Cave Art – A Classic Demonstration   72

Chapter Six
Politics Confluence of Religion and Culture for Power and Control   83

Agriculture – A Classic Demonstration   89

Conclusion	101
Glossary	105
Appendices	145
Bibliography	161
About the Author	167
Index	169

ACKNOWLEDGEMENTS

With a lifetime of study in the field, I am in a quandary as to whom not to mention as a source of my indebtedness. Much of what is said in the following exploration is owed to so many but memory fails as to whom credit is due. Let me say, then, that for any insights which are meritorious, I wish to express a blanket statement of gratitude to my teachers and colleagues, but for any misspeaks or foolishness, I assume personal responsibility. The early work of Charles Winick and his now unavailable *Dictionary of Anthropology* constituted my teething ring in this field along with the following great teachers and resources, namely, Charles Winick's *Dictionary of Anthropology* (Totowa, NJ: Littlefield, Adams & Co., 1956), William A. Haviland's *Anthropology* (NY: Holt, Rinehart and Winston, Inc., 1974), Victor Barnouw's *An Introduction to Anthropology* (Homewood, IL: The Dorsey Press, 1972), William A. Haviland's *Human Evolution and Prehistory* (NY: Holt, Rinehart & Winston, 1979), Sharon McKern and Thomas W. McKern's *Living Prehistory: An Introduction to Physical Anthropology and Archaeology.* (Menlo Park, CA: Cummings Publishing Co., 1974), Robert Bradwood's *Prehistoric Men* (Glenview, IL: Scott, Foresman & Co., 1967), William White Howells' *Evolution of the Genus* Homo (Reading, MA: Addison-Wesley Publ., 1973), S. L. Washburn and Ruth Moore's *Ape Into Man: A*

Study of Human Evolution (Boston: Little, Brown and Co., 1974), Derek Roe's *Prehistory: An Introduction* (Berkeley, CA: University of California Press, 1970), Peter Ucko and Andrée Rosenfield's *Palaeolithic Cave Art* (NY: World University Library, 1967), and David E. Hunter and Phillip Whitten's *Encyclopedia of Anthropology* (NY: Harper & Row, 1976).

To the Hartford Seminary Foundation, where I first encountered anthropology of religion under the tutelage of my teachers Robley Whitson and Bhabagrahi Misra, and to Harvard, Yale, and Princeton, where I was permitted under successive postdoctoral appointments to deepen my understanding of this fascinating field, I am eternally grateful. Along the way, both the University of Chicago and the University of Notre Dame provided me three postdoctoral appointments, each of which served as a polishing ground for my early work in the field and, finally, to Oxford University which has over the years welcomed my teaching a doctoral-level summer seminar in cognates of this subject, no expression of thanks could be comprehensively formulated to fully convey the depth of my gratitude. I would be less than gracious if I failed to say that it is due primarily to the early and enthusiastic encouragement of Clifford Geertz of Princeton's Institute for Advanced Studies that I have continued my work on this topic. If the following even suggests glimmers of his own work, it is not by accident. To him, I say thank you for the challenge and the encouragement once again.

INTRODUCTION

This inquiry is intended to explore the earliest manifestations of religious consciousness among our Paleolithic ancestors. It is not designed to be a defense of **Darwinian evolutionary science**[*] but rather embraces that science as a prerequisite to the inquiry. Furthermore, no effort will be made to be "convincing" with respect to humankind's Paleolithic origins but rather this essay takes as a scientific given our evolution from pre-human to human form.

Therefore, what we are in pursuit of here in this investigation is both a definition of "religious consciousness" which is compatible with evolutionary science and the identification and analysis of the demonstrative evidence among early humankind of a "religious sensibility." Naturally, the burden is upon the definition of "religious" consciousness and the evidence from **Paleolithic** times of such sensibilities. This is our agenda.

Definitional Constraints Within this Study

Since all argumentation with presupposition is circular, all that is demanded of us here is to state the presuppositions embodied in the terms used herein and

---

[*] Bolded words are in the Glossary and the Index.

then set about to prove the obvious. Since we presuppose the validity, indeed, indisputability, of evolutionary science, we need only re-state the presupposition as relates to our discussions of the Paleolithic Period and then move on to our presuppositions regarding religious consciousness. (*See Appendix L for primate evolution.*)

What we mean by "Paleolithic origins" is simply that expansive time period when pre-humans were beginning to populate the earth in a frantic evolutionary push towards consciousness and personhood. The Paleolithic Age covered from 1,500,000 years ago to about 20,000 years ago during which human artifacts, now found along with the bones of extinct wild animals, were produced by **flint chipping**. The Paleolithic Age, a name coined by the anthropologist Sir John Lubbock in 1865, is also called the **Middle Old Stone Age**, the **Old Stone Age**, or the **Stone Age**. It is often divided into various stages, ranging from the pre-**Chellean** to the **Magdalenian** and the **Azilian**, which constituted the transitional cultures leading up to the **Neolithic Age**. In the Paleolithic Age, human beings slowly began differentiating themselves from the animal world. We lived in small groups, perhaps often in caves, where most remains are found. Since human cultures developed at differing paces, there is considerable overlapping of these arbitrary time frames – Lower, Middle, Upper – based upon archeological and anthropological evidence of emerging human cultures throughout Europe, Asia, and Africa. For analytical purposes, nevertheless, three time frames are helpful.

The **Lower Paleolithic Period** covers the time from about 550,000 years ago to about 70,000 years ago, including the pre-Chellean, Chellean, and Acheulian stages of development. In what was sometimes called the

Old Stone Age, fire was not used during this period, nor were animals or plants domesticated. The Paleolithic peoples were simple hunters and *coup-de-posing* became smaller and smaller while more regular flakes were produced during this period. Later, tools were produced by roughing out a core so that flakes could be struck from it and made into tools by retouching. Two culture areas were discernable during this early time frame by anthropologists, viz., the Southwest-Asiatic-African-West Europe and the East-Europe and North-Asiatic.

The Middle Paleolithic Period of cultural history covers the period of the third **interglacial** through the fourth **glacial epoch**. (*See glaciation time charts in Appendix E and Appendix H.*) This period covered from about 125,000 years ago to about 20,000 years ago. From a cave in Le Moustier, France, it is also called the **Mousterian** period. This period saw the rise of **Neanderthaloids** which is sometimes called the period of the Cave Man. Flint implements appear during this time and bone tools, scraper tools, and fire were characteristic of early humans during this period. Human beings had a stable residence and buried their dead, suggesting the belief in an afterlife and religion which it is our intention to explore. Along with the dead, flints, red ocher, and uneaten cooked meat were often buried. Although the dead were buried inside the caves, the Neanderthal did not actually live deep inside, but under the overhanging ledge and on the outer platforms of these caves. There may have been a curtain of animal skins used to keep out the wind. The flint industry over most of habitable Europe became fairly uniform, as well as in nearby parts of Asia and Africa. This was the period of maximum **Würm glaciation.**

The Upper Paleolithic Period covered from about

70,000 years ago to about 20,000 years ago. It includes the **Aurignacian, Solutrean,** and **Magalenian** stages of human social and cultural development. Bone, ivory, and flint implements were used in this era. The **Cro-Magnon** people of this time had clothes made from animal skins and produced what is probably the first art. The bulk of the European Paleolithic culture was largely carried by the Cro-Magnons. Cultural diversity was probably greater than racial diversity. Long, fine knifelike flakes were also struck with care. The bow and arrow and the domestication of the dog appeared during this time period which ended with the retreat of the last glacier. Cave painting in southwest Europe began during this period and human burials with ornaments in the grave are not uncommon. The first nude statuettes of women, in stone, bone and ivory, appeared and cave paintings and figurines suggest fairly well developed religious beliefs. The last stage of the Upper Paleolithic Period is called the Magdalenian.

What we mean by "religious consciousness" is, of course, not scientifically defensible but philosophically speculative as we are bringing an interpretive grid to bear upon scientifically demonstrable evidence of a certain pattern of human behavior – artistic expression, ritualized burial, etc. The archeological verification of the presence of these artifacts cannot be disputed in any serious manner. However, the "interpretive grid" which we will be constructing and then applying to the empirical evidence can most assuredly be challenged. Nevertheless, we press on with our argument that Stone Age peoples had a consciousness of religious sensibilities. We will see that three dimensions to the human experience facilitated this sensibility, namely, early humans had the *capacity, opportunity, and inclination* needed to construct religious expression.

When we say early humans had the "capacity" for religious reflectivity, we mean the biological capability owing to brain size. Biological capacity for reflectivity was, of course, crucial in our mental development. The skulls of *Australopithecus africanus* present a generally **hominid** quality, with small brain cases and protruding, chinless jaws. (*See Appendices B and H for illustrative details.*) Within the small cranium of *Australopithecus africanus*, the brain assumes moderate proportions, varying from about 450 cc. to a maximum of nearly 700 cc. Gorilla brains run from around 300 cc. to a recorded maximum of 685 cc. while the chimpanzee-orangutan range is 290 cc. to 475 cc. The average brain of *Australopithecus africanus* is distinctly larger than that of the average chimpanzee but similar to that of gorillas. Relative to body size, however, the brain of *Australopithecus africanus* is distinctly larger than that of the massive gorilla and somewhat larger than those of the chimpanzee and orangutan. Among the several primate genera and in comparison with even lower animal forms, brain volume, **cortical surface area**, and the relative development of the different parts of the brain are determinable and are, indeed, significant indicators of relative mental capacity and degree of environmental adaptability – including, of course, the ability to produce culture. It will be seen that the higher fossil hominids all have relatively large brains; in the case of modern humans, the minimal size is 1,000 cc., whereas the largest known pathological brains run to 2,000 cc. The human mean is approximately 1,500 cc. for males and 50 cc. less for females.

The **cranial capacity** of *Australopithecus*, as we said, varied within the range of 450 cc. to 700 cc., averaging about 500 cc. The cranial capacity of *Homo erectus*, however, varied from about 775 cc. to nearly 1,300 cc., with an average of nearly 975 cubic centimeters. The upper part of that range overlaps the range for modern humans. This means that some members of **Homo erectus** had brains larger than many people living today. Evolving humans had nearly doubled their brain size within a span of only two million years. (*See illustrative details of the evolution of the skull in Appendix A.*)

Much more will be said later regarding the evolving of the fully developed human brain and the implications for the development of culture, but for now let us mention "opportunity" for religious reflection beyond the biological capacity owing to increased brain size. This is, more than anything, a "sociological" dimension to reflectivity whereas the "capacity" was more specifically a "biological" dimension of human development. The opportunity for reflection is, of course, linked to early humans' discovery and development of a manipulative capacity to control fire for their own uses. This capacity, of course, had a great impact upon dietary habits as well as living habits. With fire manipulation, our early forebears were able to inhabit caves thereby providing a safe environment for socializing, communicating, and sharing. Fire at the entrance to a cave gave them frontal safety from marauding carnivores and a safe domicile in the three sided cave for the inevitable development of familial and social nurturing behavior. Thus, in addition to the mental capacity for reflective thought, they had the environmental opportunity to enjoy communal leisure devoid of invasive fears of weather and animals.

Finally, and not inconsequentially, is the "inclination" to reflect upon human experience and to share that reflective thought in community. If capacity was biological and opportunity was sociological, then we suggest that "inclination" was psychological. Only the human animal seems to have the inclination to speculate, to imagine, to prognosticate, and to muse about the meaning and nature of life, where we came from, who we are, and where we are going. Other members of the animal kingdom seem not to have this inclination, this obsession, this desire to know more than what we are able to grasp in our encounter with the physical world, a desire to explain and interpret the environment rather than merely respond to it. (Amusingly, **theologians** would have us believe that humans have the propensity owing to our abiding thirst to be at one and at peace with our estranged god due to the Original Sin of Adam and Eve whereas animals are free of sin and, therefore, need not seek god!) Speculative musing about life, its meaning, its purpose, its direction, if such there be, has characterized the human spirit from the earliest days of storytelling and cave painting. Always the animal to interpret, indeed, we might call ourselves not just *Homo symbolicum* but more poignantly *Homo hermeneuticus* for not only are we the symbolizing animal *par excellence* but we are more decidedly the interpreting animal. Where two or three are together sharing an experience, an interpreter will emerge, the one who gives meaning and purpose to the human experience. Rather than prostitution, as is popularly supposed, we might just argue that the priesthood is, therefore, the "oldest profession."

The pre-historical parameters of our inquiry will focus upon those things we know, without argument, about early human experience. These include fire manipulation, cave dwelling, story-telling, artistic expression, leisure, culinary refinements, language acuity, and social interaction. These we have chosen to reference owing to their incontrovertibly verifiable evidence of existence as provided by archeological artifacts. These things we know were characteristic of early human beings and their communities. Much may be argued regarding human evolution, but no seriously minded person will question the archeological evidence validating the existence of these particular human activities. In some ways, these behavioral components of early human experience are part of an overall constellation in terms of their psycho-social and emotional integration. That is to say, everything about early human existence seems to center upon our developed capacity to manipulate fire, for it was with this advancement in our ability to engineer the physical environment to suit our own personal needs and desires that everything else regarding emotional, cultural, and social development occurred.

Our intention here is not to write yet another book on the evolution of the human species. That has been done well and many times over. We will embrace that work and quickly move to our specific task which is to illustrate how religious consciousness first manifested itself within the human experience as evidenced from paleo-anthropological findings among our early ancestors. To do that, we need only a brief reminder of the fundamental physical conditions under which this phenomenon of religious consciousness emerged. Obviously, there is a progressive nature to this emergence and much depended upon human physical development and adaptation.

The fundamental physical conditions necessary for the development of human consciousness include the following, not necessarily sequential but clustered to create the right environment for reflective self-awareness. Fire, of course, was primary, not just the reality of it but both the capacity to manipulate it intentionally and to eventually make it. Fire transformed early human existence, allowing for movement off the danger-ridden **savannas** with their open ground and carnivorous inhabitants and into caves. Though inhabited by saber tooth tigers and massive bears, the presence of fire in the hands of early hunters allowed for the driving out of these residents thereby making room for early people seeking both shelter from the elements and safety from the inhospitable mammalian life. By casting a bonfire in the entrance of the cave, people were safe for the first time on four sides, three sides of the cave and fire at the entrance. This was transformative for early human experience for several reasons. Certainly, for thousands of years our ancestors had been acquainted with fire; fire on the savannas could be severe and the aftermath left smoldering stumps and logs and particularly branches ready to be handled by the brave and adventurous. But to intentionally use fire for their own purposes, to make it when they liked, this took advancement in thought and technique.

Fires would have burned animal flesh on the savannas and the aroma from burning and cooking flesh could not have gone unnoticed and untasted for long by the inquisitive human animal. Flesh held over a fire for awhile both smelled and tasted better than raw meat. And, it was softer to chew and everyone, young and old alike, could partake. The protein content of flesh brought about improvement in both health and size of early peoples. Furthermore, up along the borders of the glacial caps, fire provided a welcomed source of warmth, a center of social gathering in the evening in safety for the sharing of experiences during the day on the hunt and in the camp. Besides warmth, it provided light, light which extended the day and increased the interactive time among members of the camp, young and old, when darkness shrouded the outside world. Food, safety, and society all developed rapidly due to our early abilities to create and manipulate fire.

For it was the cave, the preferred domicile of early humans, which provided the social matrix for interactive skills development, crafts, conversations, culinary refinements and artistic expression. In earlier times, we merely inhabited the entrances for shelter and protection, but later on we moved deeper into the caves for a more comfortable abode wherein time became a perceived and valued opportunity to further deepen relationships and for the sharing and cultivation of survival and hunting techniques and, indeed, medical lore.

With fire for warmth, cooked food and protection and the cave in which to enjoy them, the human community had for the first time an opportunity to enjoy leisure, an indispensable ingredient in the development of culture. For only in a time of leisure, amidst the necessities of safety and food, the human person could both turn inward personally and outward socially. Language could evolve amidst the telling of stories, first acted out with primitive gestures and grunts, but with ever increasing sophistication of sound fluctuation. The burgeoning of vocabulary necessary for the nuancing of a story of the hunt or plans for the hunt inevitably would occur. With the interplay between story and language, talking and the telling of adventures past and adventures planned for the future, leisure became the context within which human interaction could develop with ever increasing subtlety and refinement. Of course, time consciousness had emerged within the fabric of human experience and the notion of the passage of time became an integral part of story-telling. Thanks to fires and caves, leisure emerged within the human experience bringing with it the development of language. Talking became that which we did to survive and to thrive – survive on the demanding hunts and thrive within the camp community of social relationships. Young and old alike, men and women, all were the beneficiaries. The old ones could tell the stories the young ones would value and from which they could learn. And aesthetic expression followed not long behind. Cave paintings, conveying the stories of the hunt, past and planned, became both possible and necessary for the continued survival of the community. Fraught with possible incantation-laden powers and conjurings, art became both a pastime and a passion, a catechetical school for the soon to be grown youth destined for the hunt as providers of the necessities of clan life. Without fire and the cave, without leisure, language, and society, artistic expression would have been meaningless and impossible.

This is the point at which we will take up our story. We will, of course, necessarily revisit each of these fundamental ingredients to human evolution. We will emphasize their relevance in the "psycho-social expressiveness" of our humanness. We will explore their relevance to our biological, sociological, and psychological composition as interactive beings. We will recite the gifts and advancements brought about by **hominidal sequencing** from Neanderthals to *Homo sapiens sapiens*. And, we will discuss their bearing upon the emergence of religion, culture, and politics within the human experience. By doing so, we will hope to further our understanding of the emergence of religious consciousness during Paleolithic times and, thereby, will illustrate how fundamentally human religion really is. (*See taxonomic inventory of the Hominids in Appendix D.*)

Chapter One

Psycho-Social Expressiveness
(Ingredients of Humanness)

Fundamental ingredients to humanness include artistic expression, education, a sense of community, and speculation about the nature and meaning of life. Other ingredients might arguably be added to this list but these are indisputably fundamental to what we understand it means to be human. Each of these ingredients occur in consort with the others and, therefore, there is really no sequencing or prioritizing of these fundamental ingredients which make us human. The absence of any one of these would mean a diminution to a quality of existence which most would agree would be sub-human. Aesthetic expression is as essential to the human experience as speculating about the meaning of life. The sharing of information through stories, needed for survival, encouragement, insight, and instruction, is an integral part of that which makes up the human community, a place wherein the group nurtures each individual and each individual relies upon the group.

Aesthetic Expressiveness

From the earliest times during the Upper Paleolithic period (ca. 12,000 - 20,000 years ago), art has been found in the caves of southern France and northern Spain. This form of artistic expression consists of representations of animals, some of which are now extinct. As it is associated with Cro-Magnon skeletal remains it is also called Cro-Magnon Art. This form of early art consists of finger tracing, bas-relief, sculpture, painting, and engraving. Its creators probably camped on the terrace of the cave or under an overhanging rock. Because cave art is found where there is limestone, cave art is associated with blade tools in which the flake was shaped before being detached from the core, and is thus identified as Upper Paleolithic. The oldest cave art convention consists of **finger tracings** in the damp clay on certain cave walls. The earliest kind of engraving, consisting of simple outline drawings, is sometimes found over these finger tracings. Those representations developed from rough silhouettes to more precise forms and in the direction of greater realism. The animals were shown with two and then with four legs. Black and red were probably the first colors used. In some engravings the animal's body is represented by long **striations** which suggest shading. Representations of scenes or persons together, however, are rare. Changes in style occur in several areas at once so that it is likely that there were schools for the learning of painting technique.

The early cave engraving was probably accomplished by **flint burins**, which are often found associated with cave art. Natural **ochers** were frequently used to provide color. These ochers are iron oxides mixed with clay, earth, and other materials. Red, orange, yellow, and chocolate were used. Manganese oxide led to a blue-black and carbonaceous materials like burned bones provided black. Cave art did not have any green, white, or blue. The pigment was probably ground, put in shells or tubes of bone, mixed with some fatty material, and applied.

Since cave art is sometimes located far from the cave entrance, stone lamps with moss wicks burning were used to light the way to the paintings. Almost all Upper Paleolithic cave art is found in inaccessible and dark places, and this may be tied in with this art's supposed function in **propitiating** animal spirits. The frequency of artists painting pictures over earlier pictures points toward the special use of some crannies for the conjuring of power over the elements or over the hunted game. It should be pointed out, however, that we have no empirical evidence of anything like a belief in a transcendent being at this time.

What interests us here is not the speculations about the meaning and purpose of the cave art found in many different caves in many different places portraying many and varied kinds of animals and scenes. This kind of speculation we leave to the anthropologists of art and a brief bibliography of some of the more important studies is provided at the end of this book. What singularly captures our attention for purposes of our own inquiry is the fact of the artistic expression itself, not what it might mean, who did it, etc., but that it was actually done in the first place. The insuppressible human urge to express ourselves artistically is validated by these cave paintings. From the earliest of human communities during the Upper Paleolithic period, human beings living together in community, sharing caves for warmth and safety, have taken the time and gone to the effort, often at great sacrifice of time and energy, to engage in artistic portrayals of life's experiences, expectations, and speculations about life's meaning. To go beyond the necessities of survival, to intentionally contrive to express on the wall of a cave using effort-requiring instruments and concoctions, not to mention the sheer effort of access and consumption of valuable time, is indicative of the human propensity to reflectivity and intentionality. Cave art didn't just happen; human beings made it happen by design and will. This kind of expressiveness is part of what makes us human.

Survival Wisdom

Of course, we didn't just survive by accident. The level of intentionality must have been matched by knowledge of what to do and how to do it. Education was and is essential to the survival of the species and the survival of the planet. And the knowledge needed was not instinctual but rather learned. The accumulation of the folk wisdom needed for Paleolithic peoples to survive is, if we think about it, monumental. Information about clothing, food, hunting, gathering skills, medications, comfort enhancers, traveling and directional skills, all bespeak a massive storehouse of social and cultural wisdom.

Herein lies one of the strongest arguments for the necessity of nurture and care of the elderly for it is with them that the folk wisdom of survival would be entrusted. Humanity survived owing to this treasure trove of stored wisdom, survival education learned and cherished by the old for the assurance of survival of the young. Far from a tooth and claw existence, early human beings would have necessarily been nurturing, solicitous, forbearing and longsuffering with the old in hopes that the young would inherit the legacy of their corporate wisdom.

Community Development

Of course, all of this survival wisdom both required and nurtured a sense of community, a realization that the survival of the one was radically dependent upon the survival of the group. The "survival ethic" naturally would have emerged in this reality and the social and emotional nurturing of one another was quite indispensable to the survival of the family and the clan. In the absence of such **psychodynamic** nurturing, a community cannot endure. The cave provided the physical parameters for nurturing this interdependence, and the development of language and social interactive skills would have been the natural results. In order to endure, the community had to grow into an awareness of the nature and function of such interactive social skills as power brokering, social control, individual versus corporate dominance, and the multiplicity of nurturing skills needed for the benefit of the individual, the family, the clan, the old, the young, and the unhealthy. Failure of the human community to have engaged in the development of these sensitivities would have inevitably resulted in extinction. Food, clothing, and shelter were merely the outer necessities required for a much more profound development of the psycho-social dimensions of human relationships.

Speculation (Religion in the Making)

Art, education, and community were, of course, fundamental ingredients in the emergence of the human person and society. Within this context, fostered by fire and occurring within the cave, artistic expression, survival lore, and the development of group social skills constituted the framework within which those who were so inclined could indulge that uniquely human propensity to musings upon the meaning and nature, purpose and direction of human life. The only animal, apparently, to intentionally engage in such an enterprise, namely, speculating about life, was the human animal and, therefore, the earliest human communities necessarily and inevitably played host to the resident philosopher. Speculation is singularly a human inclination and, as was once said millennia ago, for the human person, "the unexamined life is not worth living."

In recognition of those strikingly obvious human propensities to both rationality (finding the reason for things) and for hope (believing that the future can and should be better), philosophers in the form of story tellers, later to become priests, emerged. Musing upon the verities of life and the unknown, that which we know and recognize as our own mortality and musing upon that which we do not know seems early and clearly to have been an occupation of Paleolithic peoples. Witness the emergence of ritualistic burial of the dead and the graphic cave art as dual illustrations of the point.

Of course, who these first philosophers (who eventually became priests) were is an interesting speculative enterprise in itself. Certainly, the capacity to manipulate language would have been crucial and, thus, the most verbal would have been the most likely to fill this communal function. Furthermore, those with the capacity to draw from past personal experience such as the hunt would be well positioned to embellish to their own aggrandizement and to the fascination of the audience as well. Finally, the oldest person who would have the longest memory as well as the greatest number of stories would rise to the occasion as the community philosopher or storyteller. The telling of the communal stories, of course, carries with it the opportunity and the enticement to power and control for by telling the story one could direct and manipulate the story and its message to suit oneself. To control the story is to control the power.

Chapter Two

Tripartite Matrix of Evolution
(Biological capacity, Sociological opportunity, Psychological inclination)

The ingredients of humanness, namely, art, education, community, and religion, manifest themselves within the context of the physical, social, and emotional environment created through the evolutionary process. This process is composed of three interrelated components – biology, sociology, and psychology. More specifically, the emergence of the human animal as an individual and as a social being is dependent upon the evolving of a "biological capacity" for survival, the "sociological opportunity" to sustain and nurture social life, and the "psychological inclination" to both reflect upon and articulate those musings for the benefit of the community. This evolutionary process, or organic emergence, will be discussed here as **biogenesis, sociogenesis,** and **psychogenesis.**

Biogenesis
Bipedalism / Stereoscopic Vision / Verbal Acuity / Opposable Digitation

In the previous chapter we mentioned in passing that capacity, opportunity, and inclination were necessary for the human community, during the Paleolithic period, to emerge and thrive. And, when we speak of capacity, we specifically refer to "biological" capacity with reference not just to brain size, discussed earlier, but also the development of **bipedalism, stereoscopic vision, verbal acuity**, and **opposable digitation** which, specifically, is needed for the creation and use of tools. Without delving into the nuancing of time sequencing, that is, such valid but presently irrelevant questions as which came first and what came later, we are fully aware that the emergence of the human community was radically dependent upon the human individual's capacities to walk upright, to see three dimensionally, to speak with clarity and precision, and to use the hand with skill and precision. (*See illustrative details in Appendix I.*) These biological capabilities were indispensable in the evolutionary process of human emergence and survival.

The "standing upright" posture constituted a monumental evolutionary advance over **quadrupedal locomotion**. (*See Appendix O for illustrative details.*) This shifting from four legs to two, from periodic walking upright to a permanent stance is traced through hundreds of thousands of years until we reach an established bipedalism. The releasing of the arms and hands for gathering, while walking, was enormously important. Furthermore, the capacity to throw things evolved and the skills developed in the making of tools could only occur when the arms and hands were freed from locomotion. Frontal and facial interaction with other humans was facilitated by bipedalism whereas before the horizontal posture failed to inculcate eye-contact when frontally encountering another member of the band. One of many behavioral dynamics altered by this frontal encountering brought on by bipedalism was sexual selection and intercourse which shifted from a posterior to a primarily frontal positioning. This introduced the psycho-social dimensions of mating and mate selection not available in quadrupedalism. Speed of locomotion, not unimportant on the savannas where predators are everywhere, was greatly enhanced when we moved from walking on all fours to bipedalism. Carrying of food and needed survival items such as weapons and hunting implements, and most importantly, the capacity to run fast while holding a young one all contributed to the further development of social life among early human animals, and was all due to the evolution of standing upright and walking on two legs.

Furthermore, **stereoscopic vision** evolved in relationship to the development of the skull and this occurred extremely early in the long history of hominidal evolution. To see three dimensionally with two frontal eyes dates from the evolution of the **simians** and continued to both develop and complement the evolution of the human animal. Crucial for the capacity to "objectify" an item, such as tools, stereoscopic vision was a great advancement over eyes placed at the sides of the head which see landscapes, for example, as two-dimensional flat sheets, able only to detect what moves across a plain field but not items holding still or moving directly towards one, such as a stalking tiger. The structure of the monkey brain reflected these changes. The cortex expanded considerably, perhaps about two or three times, burying most of the old **smell-brain centers**. The diminishment of the **olfactory sense** is directly correlated with the increase in the visual capacity of the brain, all based on space available within the skull. Although a large part of the expansion involved the visual cortex at the back of the brain, other areas were affected, such as certain areas concerned with the control of finger movements – a tiny strip of cortex on the right side of the brain, for example, controls the fingers of the left hand, a corresponding left-side strip the right hand. The degree of detail on the map of the cortex depends on the evolutionary status of the species, i.e., the more developed the species, the greater the refinement in digital dexterity!

Though bipedalism and stereoscopic vision were crucial in our development, not enough can be said regarding the development of our verbal acuity. Speech is the biologically refining mechanism which facilitated our development into a reflective thinking being. This biological capacity, the ability to articulate and manipulate a wide range of sounds, with intentioned conveyance of meaning between human individuals was an early development contributing to our survival. The physical deficiencies of human anatomy were greatly minimized owing to our developing capacity to communicate verbally with precision and comprehension which was valuable for the great hunt as well as for domestic interaction within the family, the community, and between individuals. The development of **myth** through story-telling was only possible due to the development of verbal communication skills, and the more refined the verbal skills, the more elaborate the stories. And, to be sure, the more refined the communication the greater the opportunity to develop and elaborate whole systems of thought, ideas, rules, etc.

Finally, within the context of the biogenesis of the human animal generally, we must address specifically the fundamental skills of digital dexterity needed for the making of tools for survival and for the enhancement of the quality of life among early peoples. Called **opposable digitation**, the capacity to oppose the thumb to the fingers and to bring the fingertips into contact with the ball of the thumb, is a defining characteristic of the human hand which distinguishes the human species from all other primates, prehistoric and modern. (*See illustrative details in Appendix M.*) The human hand is capable of two major types of grips. In the **power grip**, an object is held between the fingers and the palm, with the thumb reinforcing the fingers. In this position, much force can be applied. All primates are capable of the power grip.

The **precision grip**, however, is used when an object is held between one or more fingers with the thumb fully opposed to the fingertips. Very delicate movements can be executed in this position. Humans have developed the precision grip to a degree not found in other primates, granted chimps and other pongids do exercise a degree of precision in finger/thumb opposition such as in using a straw to extricate ants from a bed for feeding. The precision of the human animal in the use of the hand through oppositional thumb/finger dexterity is unprecedented in the primate world.

We can summarize the evolution of the human hand by marking two stages in its development. First, the primate **arboreal environment** selects the opposable thumb, for grasping branches, and this thumb appears among the **prosimians** and in turn makes possible manipulation among **Old World Monkeys** but not present among **New World Monkeys**. Second, the ecological move to the open plains correlated with bipedalism frees the hand from all locomotor functions and allows the perfection of the precision grip by some minor modifications of the thumb. The hand has contributed as much as the eye to the making of the human animal; together they gave the human animal a new perception of the environment and, with technology, a new control of it. From chipped stone ware to pottery to sewing to typing, the human animal has maximized the evolution of the hand to further the biogenesis of the human species.

The biological capacities of walking upright, seeing three dimensional objects, verbally expressing thought, and the making of tools all contribute to human survival and, even more, to the thriving of the human community against all odds.

Sociogenesis
Social Interaction / Linguistic Acuity / Socio-dynamic Connectedness

But, in addition to biological capacity, early humans necessarily had to evolve social interaction skills, linguistic acuity, and a sense of the dynamics of social connectedness. Brain size alone was certainly not enough, not even walking upright on two feet, not even an increased ability to manipulate the tongue and pallet for verbal sophistication, or the unique capacity to finger each digit with the thumb. No, beyond these biological capacities, sociological opportunity had to emerge and be utilized. Beyond biogenesis, sociogenesis was essential in the development of the human person and the human community.

Of course, there is no evolutionary sequencing here. That is, we are not suggesting that first came the biological capacity and then the social opportunity. Rather they evolved concurrently, simultaneously feeding off of each other, stimulating and provoking development towards reflectivity and consciousness. The physical body was complimented by the corresponding socialization skills resulting and benefiting from new biological capabilities. Interaction, language, and sociality were, of course, the fundamental ingredients in the emergence of the human community — person-to-person interaction, families, clans. All three benefited from the push towards bipedalism, stereoscopic vision, digital dexterity, and verbal communication.

The hunt, the camp, and the person all constituted the socially interactive matrix for skill development. Food from the hunt was indispensable, and the more successful the hunt, the greater the benefit to the community and, therefore, the greater the likelihood of survival. In order to assure hunting success, socially interactive communication was crucial - visual and verbal. The increasing capacity to work together, as a unit, as a concerted corporate effort towards a single mutually beneficial goal, characterized the hunt. Men and boys collaborating, coordinating, communicating, and executing the effort is what made human survival possible. Within this matrix, the interactive skills of refined and finessed communication capabilities were enhanced by the opportunity for such made possible by cave dwelling, fire manipulation, and the attractiveness of collegiality. Only *Homo soloensis* (Solitary Man) attempted but failed to live apart. The human experience is one of collegiality, sociality, mutuality, and cooperation. These are the traits that assured our survival.

Though indispensable, verbal capability was not enough for we needed to evolve linguistic acuity, a capacity to continually refine and finesse our verbal and non-verbal communication skills. The subtle inflexion of intonations coupled and complemented with facial, hand, and body gesticulations all conspired to facilitate the nuancing of message conveyance. The hunt was very dangerous but absolutely necessary. The loss of life was inevitable; the sustaining of life was the challenge and the better the communication, verbal and non-verbal, the greater the chances of survival. The camp that communicated the best survived, even thrived, in the face of indeterminate odds and incalculable eventualities. The pressure socially for the continual refinement of language was tremendous.

But beyond social interactive skills and linguistic acuity, the capacity to identify with and relate to the social dynamic of community, a sense of corporate connectedness was necessary and inevitable. In the hunt, in the camp, within the bosom of the social family, every individual was a valuable member, a contributing partner in the great struggle to survive. The elderly provided the repository of survival wisdom regarding food sources and preparations, medical condiments, migration histories, and animal lore. Infants and youth provided the basis for hope for tomorrow to carry on the social life of the community. The skill to read a face, to detect the subtleties of a gesture, the necessity of judging a comment, all converged within the social matrix for survival and perpetuity. Those more skilled at reading the signs – faces and gestures and sounds and silences of each member – were those destined to lead, to direct, to counsel, and to confront. From within this rising cluster of socially astute members of the community came the eventual leaders, shamans, priests, teachers, great hunters, and all patriarchs and matriarchs of the cave dwellers.

But it was the social opportunity rather than the biological capacity that made human survival possible. The opportunity of social interactive skills development occurred by virtue of life in the caves, with fire, and with language. The opportunities for social skills development, linguistic refinements, and a sense of the socially dynamic connectedness of each member of the community could only occur within the great caves of central and southern Europe and the Fertile Crescent. Everywhere fire and shelter were needed for survival and utilized, there the human animal thrived. For it was around the camp fires at night, after the hunt, after the meal, when the human family gathered together to affirm their connectedness, their collegial investment of mutuality in survival, that social life began to grow and thrive, to evolve and elaborate.

Psychogenesis
Reflective Self-awareness / Reflexive Cognition / Psychodynamic Expressiveness

With the convergence of biological capacities and sociological opportunities for the appearance of human society, there was the inevitable need for the ingredients of psychogenesis, viz., reflective self-awareness of the individual, reflexive cognition for systematic thought and analysis, and expressiveness. Individual and social relational traits such as a sense of fear, anger, compassion, empathy, sympathy, jealousy, competition, and amorous propensities were all needed for the melding of social cohesiveness within the family, clan, and community. And, we must eventually explore in some detail the human inclination to speculate for this "speculative inclination" can be argued to be the most defining characteristic of the human animal.

The balancing matrix of human evolution consists of biogenesis, sociogenesis, and psychogenesis. The biological capacity, the sociological opportunity, and the psychological inclination all conspired to produce the human animal. We are not interested in fruitless attempts to identify human characteristics which set us apart from the rest of the animal kingdom but rather to identify those specifically defining traits which make us *Homo sapiens sapiens* rather than some other species of primate. That's all. Nothing more is needed for, in doing so, we isolate and elevate those traits of "humanness" for examination in our quest for the Paleolithic origins of religious consciousness. Later we will see that we are not merely *Homo habilis* (tool maker) but also *Homo hermeneuticus* (interpreter). We not only make things, we interpret our environment and our experiences.

This imperative to interpret in order to understand is indicative of our rise to consciousness. By consciousness we mean "reflective self awareness." We feel fear, we are aware that we feel fear, and we are aware that we feel compelled to explore, identify, and explain the fear we feel. Reflective self-awareness is a defining characteristic of the human experience; what it means to be human. Though chickens experience fear, they don't write books about it or make movies about it. We do. And it is an inclination which has characterized the human animal from earliest times, from the time of the cave dwellers when members of the community felt compelled to express their experience through the medium of cave art. Reflexive cognition is a personal awareness that we think and that we think about thinking and that we know we think about thinking. Thinking about thinking is what we do, and then acting upon that thought process, that which results from this self-reflective awareness and this reflexive cognition, is the eventual outcome.

This kind of socially validated psychodynamic expressiveness is both encouraged and validated by the community. The community looks to the leaders whom they know have thought through the agenda -- the task at hand, the hunt, the migration, the occupation or abandonment of a domicile. The community is confident that the leaders have engaged in this kind of reflection, and that the resulting decision will be of benefit to them all. Likewise, when these individuals vested by the community with confidence in thinking, planning, and acting, take the initiative, they do so with the community's support. When they react to, inculcate, or provoke fear or anger or hope, they do so with the social mandate of the community. All such action, based on reflection, grows out of a need for and value of speculation; and the inclination to speculate about the unknown, the future, the possibilities, is a defining characteristics of the human species. Those more inclined rather than less inclined to speculate, reflect, cogitate, muse, and then plan and act are destined to lead. Herein lies the necessity for the human community to identify those with the aptitude to lead and then to determine to follow those so identified.

Chapter Three

Hominidal Sequencing
(Aptitude Development)

The Branching:
Survival based on ever-increasing Skills Aptitude

There are many different and legitimate bases on which we could plot the emergence of modern persons and societies from our Paleolithic origins. Any given physical trait or cultural characteristic could be used and each would prove effective within its own parameters of analysis. Yet, from the perspective taken in our investigation, reflective aptitude constitutes the most relevant measure of human development.

Hominids is the common name for those **hominoid**s referred to as the taxonomic family Hominidae (modern humans and their nearest evolutionary predecessors). The only living representatives of the Hominidae are all members of the single genus and species *Homo sapiens* ("wise man"). The essence of the overall adaptive pattern of hominids is often characterized as being sociocultural or extra somatic adaptation but, of course, the framework of this pattern is deeply rooted in **hominid** biology. Adoption of a fully erect posture with bipedal locomotion, coupled with enhanced manipulation by the digits of the hand, remodeling of the dentition plus associated jaw and facial structures, and the development of an elaborate and complex brain – these constitute the principal morphological evolutionary transformations of hominids. The most commonly accepted modern taxonomic designations for fossil hominids are *Homo sapiens neanderthalensis*, *Homo erectus*, *Australopithecus africanus*, *Australopithecus boisei*, and *Ramapithecus*.

Though sub-gradations could be explored *ad nauseum*, here in our treatment of the Paleolithic period we will confine our overarching discussion of "hominidal sequencing" to a consideration of the Neanderthals (*Homo neanderthalensis*), the Cro-Magnons, and the Moderns (*Homo sapiens sapiens*).

Neanderthal

Homo neanderthalensis (or, more fully, *Homo sapiens neanderthalensis*) has many variations, often divided into four subgroups, the Rhodesian group (*Homo Rhodensiensis*), the **Mousterian**, the **Ehringsdorf**, and the subgroup closest to modern people, including the Skhul Mount Carmel and the Galilee remains. *Homo neanderthalensis* was first found in Gibraltar in 1848 and was first extensively studied in 1936. It was named in 1864 by William King. Elements of over 100 Neanderthal remains have been found. It flourished during the third and fourth glacial periods. (According to Neuner, the four distinct glaciations began respectively at 600,000 years ago, 500,000 years ago, 250,000 years ago, and 120,000 years ago with this period ending about 20,000 years ago). This would put Neanderthal thriving during the period of time between ca. 250,000 and 20,000 years ago which admits of a significant period of nearly 20,000 years of overlapping with *Homo sapiens sapiens*. **Classic Neanderthals** are probably from the fourth glacial advance. Their dead were buried, along with their tools. The presence of speech may be inferred. Mousterian culture predominated. Primarily because they buried their dead and because they lived fairly recently, predominantly between 100,000 and 50,000 years ago, a good deal is known about Neanderthals. The brain of Neanderthals was probably slightly larger than the contemporary human brain and the skull longer and wider than any contemporary human type. The skull is broad behind the ears, and the back of the head protrudes. The head is not balanced and does not have a large forehead. The nose was probably large. There was little **prognathism** and not much of a chin. The mouth was large and the face was puffed around the nose. Neanderthals stood an average height of 5 feet 3 inches; the posture was stooping, with the knees semi flexed. Neanderthals' teeth were robust and their bones were heavy and thick and their joints large. Although the feet were generally human, the big toe was not separated from the other toes.

They are believed to have possessed language, a sense of community and social organization, and a belief in religion (as revealed in their burials). They collected vegetable foods and hunted mainly the herbivores, including the mammoths. They knew how to make fire and had a **flint-knapping** technique, called **Levalloisian-Mousterian**, which surpasses in excellence the stone craft of some modern primitives. Two varieties of Neanderthals are generally recognized – the "classic" or "cold-adapted" Neanderthals and the "progressive" or more modern-appearing Neanderthals. Some investigators believe *Homo sapiens sapiens* or modern humans evolved from the latter.

In many ways, Neanderthal had a number of apelike characteristics. Thus, while Neanderthal has simian limb features, fairly modern limb bones were found as long ago as **Pithecanthropus**, in Pleistocene times. It is now believed by many leading authorities that Neanderthals were not an intermediate step in *Homo sapiens'* evolution but an evolutionary sideline in which some features were exaggerated. Some of these features, like the brow ridges and **taurodontism**, are unique. A number of the earlier Mousterian specimens, when chronologically studied, have fewer Neanderthal characteristics than later Neanderthals, so that these early forms are nearer *Homo sapiens* than the later ones. There are no post-Mousterian remains that show a transition to modern man, suggesting that the extreme or classic Neanderthals may have become extinct as early as 70,000 years ago. Neanderthal's brain being larger than modern man's, it is difficult to see how it fits in with the general development of the human brain.

It has been suggested that the development of Pithecanthropus' brain led to a generalized Neanderthal, with two kinds of development around Acheulian times. These had a large brain and large brow ridges, jaws, and palate, with specialized skull and teeth, and limb changes, which gave rise to the extreme Neanderthal. The other development saw the brain being enlarged while the brow ridges and jaws receded, the teeth became smaller, and vertical forehead, and rounded cranium, appeared, as well as the limb characteristics of earlier Pithecanthropus. It is suggested that this line of development led from the Acheulians to *Homo sapiens*.

Cro-Magnon

The Cro-Magnons appeared in western Europe and are associated with the Aurignacian and later cultures of the region. Remains were first found in 1868 in the rock shelter of Cro-Magnon in the village of Les Eyzies, Dordogne, France. (Cro-Magnon is French for great holes.) Five skeletons were found there, although similar findings have been made in other regions of Western Europe. It is believed that the Cro-Magnons were absorbed into later populations. The skeletal remains of the individuals found at Dordogne in France were modern in form, and geologists were on hand to verify the age of about 20,000 to 30,000 years ago and stratigraphy of the site verified their findings as well. Cro-Magnon represents the first authoritatively documented modern human fossil remains and indicates that the various Upper Paleolithic tool traditions were the products of people like modern humans. This type was fairly tall and had a larger cranial capacity than modern man, with a high forehead and prominent chin. Cro-Magnon is probably the prehistoric *Homo sapiens* of whom we know the most. Their culture went through the **Aurignacian**, **Solutrean**, and **Magdalenian** stages. There were many stone instruments, and flint chipping reached its highest development. Reindeer horn, bone, and ivory were also used to make various implements. Cro-Magnon dwellings were in rock shelters and caves, where the dead were buried. Red ocher was found in many graves, although the exact significance of this is not known. Ornaments such as necklaces were in the graves of the period, and the fine arts, including painting, drawing, and sculpture, probably first appeared in the Aurignacian period.

Homo Sapiens Sapiens

This is the species to which all extant humans belong. First found in the Upper Paleolithic, the skull is thin-walled and the face light-boned. The forehead is high and the head dome-shaped. The hair is thrown into high relief because the face is pulled in under the forehead. There are **cheek hollow**s not found in Neanderthals and a pronounced chin. *Homo sapiens* appeared with Aurignacian culture, in which flint blades were the most important tools. In the middle of the Upper Paleolithic, *Homo sapiens* entered the Solutrean period, characterized by excellent flint working. The Magdalenian period, which followed, saw the slight deterioration of stonework and the rise of bone for tools.

In Europe, *Homo sapiens* with their Aurignacian culture probably drove the Mousterian Neanderthals away. It is possible that there were **Negroid** and **Mongoloid** elements present, in addition to some Australian elements. The races of today were probably present by the last glaciation, although they all probably had rugged and large crania. This branch in human evolution, *Homo sapiens*, is distinguished primarily by a mean cranial capacity of about 1,300 cc. Most other characteristics are variably defined by comparison with *Homo erectus*. (*See illustrative details in Appendix K.*) For example, reduced **maxillary prognathism** is linked with reduction in the use of **masticatory apparatus**; **supraorbital tori** are also variable but less pronounced than *Homo erectus*; the canines are reduced and **molar**

dentition is smaller; **postorbital constriction** is reduced and is entirely absent in contemporary populations; inflated, rounded frontal, **occipital aspects** coincide with increased brain volume, especially among modern populations.

Fossil remains attributed to *Homo sapiens* can be dichotomized arbitrarily into (1) specimens temporally and morphologically intermediate between *Homo erectus sensu lato* and Neanderthal *sensu lato*; (2) Neanderthal and "Neanderthaloid" populations, defined by consensus and on temporal criteria as *Homo sapiens neanderthalensis*; and (3) fossil representatives of morphologically modern human as *Homo sapiens sapiens*. It is important to bear in mind that a continuum is involved – the categories are not discontinuous with sharp breaks between them. Membership in the first group is most controversial because its taxonomic status is tenuous and hotly debated. Major fossils include the Swanscombe (England) and Steinem (Germany) crania; "pre-Neanderthal" specimens from Caune de l'Arago, Le Lazaret, and Fontéchevade (France); the morphologically primitive but comparatively late (early Upper Pleistocene) series from the Ngandong Beds (*Homo soloensis* of Java); the Vertesszollos and Broken Hill remains (Hungary, Zambia), and Omo crania I and II (Ethiopia). These fossils represent morphologically variable populations within a single, **polytypic species**. They do not imply (as has sometimes been argued) the survival of multiple pre-sapiens lines. They are all of probable Middle/Upper Pleistocene boundary date (approximately 250,00 to l00,00 years ago). The second group contains hominid fossils of early/middle Upper **Pleistocene** age dating from before 100,000 to 40,000 years ago; it is generally referred to as Neanderthal or Neanderthaloid. Usually included are crania and postcranial remains from Neanderthal and other sites in Germany, Greece, France, Belgium, Gibraltar, Italy, Israel, Uzbekistan, Iraq, and East Africa. The last group comprises fossil representatives of morphologically modern humans. Membership is determined by association with Upper Paleolothic archeological assemblages and/or an age of less than 40,000 years ago to as recent as 20,000 years ago. Included are skeletal remains from Paviland in England, Brno and Predmost in the Czech Republic, and other widely disparate sites in France, Italy, Iran, Java, China, and North, East and South Africa.

Of course, all of this is to say that the sequencing of hominidal development from our special interest perspective has to do primarily with "aptitude" of the emerging members of the species. We have been suggesting all along that the emergence of "religious consciousness" within the Paleolithic period of our development is directly linked to and indicative of "aptitude" of our ancestors with respect to reflective self-awareness, reflexive cognition, and expressiveness within the confines of our biological capacities, our sociological opportunities, and our psychological inclinations. In each successive developmental stride forward towards fully human consciousness, all was linked to the aptitude of the individual and community determined by biological, sociological, and psychological constraints and capabilities. Beyond the "branching" phenomenon of *Homo sapiens*, Neanderthals, and Cro-Magnons, there was the inevitable necessity of reflectivity, intentioned thought, and purposeful motivation.

Ideology and Behavior
(The Vortex of Thought and Action)

An aptitude for reflection, for thinking and planning, for speculating and musing about the unknown, as we have discussed earlier, precipitated both the capacity and propensity to cultivate "ideas," thought constellations interrelated so as to imply intentionality and purpose, direction and objectives. Ideas without behavior come to naught, so the development of ideology resulted in action by design.

Ideas and attitudes feed off of each other and both result from time apart from task-oriented activity. Ideas come and attitudes are formed all within the framework of reflection upon real experiences and anticipated experiences. Before the cave, before fire, before leisure, time was used to survive, nothing more. We have no evidence of any significant expressiveness in the form of aesthetics prior to dwelling in caves warmed by the glow of the campfire protecting the entrance and lighting the interior. But from that period forward, there was no holding human expressiveness back – cave painting, personal cosmetics, artistic expression on weapons, tools, burial sites exploded exponentially. Within this framework of heart and hearth, light, warmth and protection, within the matrix of socialization, leisure nurtured culture. Culture, as we have been saying here, is expressive of ideas, attitudes, thoughts swelling up within the context of free time and musings about the future, the unknown, the "what ifs" and "why nots" of possibility. "Possibility thinking" is what one might call it – ideas feeding imagination and attitudes growing under the light of considered opportunities.

Not all was hunting, surviving, fighting the elements, escaping the predators. Not everything was about the basics, not after the cave, not after fire. And these ideas, about what might be over the mountain, around the bend, what is there that we have yet to encounter, these things fostered "action," the "deed" being done following the idea being thought. And in the doing of a thing, character began to develop, within the individual, within the family, within the clan. Traits of conduct, quality of engagement, tendencies in the face of danger, opportunity, adventure, all of these things began to characterize the human animal. No longer tied to a pre-consciousness of survival instincts, the human animal individually and collectively began to fuse ideas and attitudes with action and character.

This was the point in our evolution when the catalytic threshold of self-awareness converged with intentionality, motivation, emotion, and imagination. We became more than we were by virtue of our capacity to think, to think about thinking, and to know that we were thinking, planning, imagining. Cognizance of memory fostered tradition; acceptance of graded skills nurtured leadership; recognition of controlled behavior stimulated the rise of law. Beyond instinct, beyond survival, beyond natural selection, the human animal was flung, or jumped, headlong into the vortex of thought and action. We became masters of ourselves, our environment, our future. Social control characterized our relationships, dominance and nurturance played a balancing role in community cooperation and in collegial cohesion.

Memory and Imagination
(Storytelling as Survival Conveyance)

Flowing freely and easily from ideology and behavior is the inevitability of remembered stories and imagined adventures. Memory and imagination are crucial to our survival and in the telling of stories lies the conveyance of information needed for survival. Power, influence, and control all are derivatives of memory and imagination for in the telling of the story lies the capacity to create, broker, distribute, hoard power, influence and control the listener and the family, the clan, and the community.

Whereas memory, and knowledge that we possess memory, offered reassurance of our survival, imagination induced audacity towards the future. By partnering memory of the past and imagination towards the future, early humans controlled the development of a world of power, influence, and control, traits and capacities for good and ill, for the welfare of the community as well as for its potential downfall. Memory and imagination were merged in the form of storytelling and herein lies the eventuality of religious consciousness. For it is in the telling of stories that the past is reconstructed and the future is envisioned for the present generation of listeners. Memory and imagination fuse the past and the future into the present moment of the telling of the stories. Sitting around the campfires in the warmth and light of the protected caves, the stories of past adventures and future prospects were told and the teller of the tales was, without doubt, conjuring the power, peddling the influence, and mongering the control as only the spinner of tales can.

Fundamentally Human Propensities

And in the memory and imagination, in the ideology and action, even in the differentiation of survival aptitude skills reside those fundamentally human traits of a quest for rationality and the pursuit of a hope for the future. These are fundamental human characteristics, all deriving from the inevitabilities of hominidal sequencing – the more human, the more rational and the more hopeful. The existential resignation of a **Kierkegaard** is not essentially a human trait but that of a slaughter animal, the pig awaiting dissection, the cow awaiting butchering, the chicken awaiting decapitation. No, the human tendency is to seek the reason for things and to find cause for hope in the future. **Sartre**, not Kierkegaard, had it right – we are condemned to freedom, but, nevertheless, we are truly free, free to reason, free to hope.

Chapter Four

Religion
How a Community Handles Awe, Wonder, and Reverence

Herbert Spencer's Unknown and Unknowable

At the risk of appearing to veer off the intended path set for this book at the beginning, I feel it imperative to offer up a philosophical foundation for our continued discussion of the emergence of religious consciousness. And it is to **Herbert Spencer** (1820-1903) that we turn for a philosophical perspective established and embraced by Darwin in the same century.

The significant points of Spencer's comprehensive philosophy are to be found in his *First Principles* (1862) and the six-part *Principles of Ethics* (1879-1893). He began by accepting the view of William Hamilton and John Stuart Mill, namely, that knowledge is concerned strictly with empirical subject matter. However, he did not take this to mean that we are inevitably involved in some form of **solipsism**, for he was much too practical and perceptive to fall into that trap. In agreement with Kant, Spencer acknowledged the existence of two domains of knowledge, that which we name "experience" and that which has traditionally been named "reality." The experience we undergo is the result of the interaction between reality and the practical human organism, but even though we are required to acknowledge the existence of the external stimulant, we can never know exactly what it is like in its own right. This is a unique case in that, although we can investigate the effects of the stimulant, the cause is inherently unknowable.

The Unknown (The triumph of scientific inquiry)

This theory of **epistemology** was found by Spencer and his followers, as well as his detractors, to be particularly applicable to religious knowledge. Since we cannot know the nature of reality apart from its effects encountered in experience, we are led to a belief in some **Unknowable**; this does not mean, however, that we are committed to a belief in the existence of a personal God. First of all, our complete dependence on sensory data for knowledge makes it impossible for us to tell whether this Unknowable is at all comparable to any kind of divine substance. We are never in the position to test whether our idea of what the Absolute is corresponds to what it actually is. Second, reasoning (which for Spencer is no more than an advanced physical ability by which an organism can meet environmental problems) cannot cope with data that are not reducible to observables. When such an endeavor is made, reasoning, like any machine whose function is abused, breaks down inevitably.

Consider what occurs when we attempt to analyze a concept whose reference is taken to be necessarily outside of the domain of experience – the concept of God, for instance. All questions are either unanswerable or produce paradoxes. If there is a God, then how did he come into existence? If he was created by something else, then who created that? And so forth into an infinite regress. Could God have created himself? If so, then out of what elements did he create himself? If there were elements out of which he created himself, then who created these elements? If he created himself out of nothing, then how can something come out of nothing? None of these questions can be answered by an appeal to some possible empirical datum, nor can they be answered by any pure logical analysis without at once involving further unanswerable questions and, ultimately, nonsense. Thus, for Spencer, theism fails as a means of giving us insight into the nature of the Unknowable and its religion. Likewise, pantheism also fails because it treats the concept of God as an immanent rather than an external power and, thus, does not eliminate the questions that are raised with theism.

The Unknowable
(The triumph of religious explanation)

Are we then necessarily led to atheism by this Spencerian epistemology? Spencer denies this as well. The fact that we do not know whether a God exists does not mean that, therefore, no god does exist. The rejection of theism and pantheism means only that we can have no empirically verifiable knowledge of or about the Unknowable, not that the Unknowable does not exist. At most we can simply say that we do not know whether there is a God or not. **Agnosticism**, Spencer concludes, is the only reasonable position in regard to religious and metaphysical issues in the world of comprehensive synthetic thinking.

Spencer, therefore, rejects all known theological schemes and was also highly critical of the various absurdities and abuses he believed existed in all religious institutions. Many religions, he claimed, still cling to beliefs that arose strictly because of wrong inferences about natural phenomena. Thus, the notion of a soul, or of a ghost, arose because primitive peoples could not account for dreams, shadows, and reflections. All such phenomena led to the belief that people were dual personalities, one of which remains unchanged regardless of changes in the visible person.

From this conception there gradually developed the theory that there were eternal, unchanging, omnipotent personalities. In this way, Spencer declared, people came to believe in gods; and, for similar reasons, the Judaeo-Christian God has many strictly human traits. Spencer deplored this religious anthropomorphism which depicted God as filled with hatred and desires that were appropriate only to human beings. He also strongly disapproved of the attempt by the church to fight scientific doctrines, especially those of Copernicus and Darwin. But, in spite of these objections, he felt that religions could serve as a means of fostering friendship and cooperation among human beings and also of guaranteeing the retention of the most worthwhile values of the past. The hope of heaven and the fear of hell are both sound incentives to good behavior. Furthermore, religion could be useful as a way of developing interest in the various enigmas that are found in the universe, a means of motivating individuals to initiate scientific inquiries, a movement, if you will, from superstition to scientific knowledge driven on by the passions fostered by religion and realized in science.

Scientific knowledge was, of course, the objective in

the comprehensive work of Spencer. The fact that we can never know what the Unknowable is in itself does not imply, according to Spencer, that we cannot have any genuine knowledge at all. The domain of phenomena is characterized by features which are not controllable by our desires or even by our manipulations. Certain relationships consistently appear in spite of our objections or antagonistic attitudes. These aspects of reality are manifestations of the Unknowable, and information about them is the only kind of knowledge human beings can obtain or ought to seek. Spencer was keen for the scientific community to identify and name the parameters within which it could do its work.

It is clear in Spencer's work that knowledge, for human beings, is not a study of the Unknowable among phenomena – he discounted the viability of a "scientific" theology studying God! (Henry Nelson Wieman and the whole "natural or empirical theology" movement to which John Macquarrie made a substantial contribution was strictly and summarily dismissed!) Rather, the scientific agenda is the study of the "manifestations" of the Unknowable among phenomena, the world of observation and experience. Out of this concern with phenomena and the force implicit in them arises science, which, according to Spencer, is simply a more sophisticated, more precisely stated form of ordinary knowledge. Science is ordinary knowledge with intentioned carefulness controlled by logic. The task of science, then, is to accumulate data and then to discover general laws, accomplishing this task by assigning the investigation of specific aspects of phenomena to specific disciplines.

Thus, says Spencer, the study of matter is the purpose of physics, and from this discipline has come the recognition of those universal characteristics of force which are described in the laws of the conservation of energy, the indestructibility of matter, and gravitation. Similarly, the science of biology studies living beings and has discovered laws of development and evolution. The other sciences have made analogous discoveries. But we ought not to think that these laws are simple empirical generalizations, for they describe the ways in which the Unknowable makes its appearance in the phenomenal world. Therefore, says he, these observable and experienced phenomena have an urgency, a necessity attached to them that is not to be found in ordinary, purely statistical laws. Thus, even though Spencer began by adopting a Kantian position, unlike Kant, he did not attribute the necessary relationships that are taken to be in nature to the peculiar formation of the human mind. These are not categorical imperatives! They are manifestations of the Unknowable in observable and experienced form.

We do not, Spencer argues, impose forms and categories on what is observed. On the contrary, the external stimulant itself imposes upon us restrictions and limitations which we cannot ignore or change. Newton's laws are not characteristic of our kind of mind, for surely we can conceive of a world in which other laws would hold and, after sufficient time, would seem to be just as necessary. We can also imagine minds being changed by operations or accidents, but such changes do not entail an accompanying reconstruction of nature. Thus, if there are any necessary relationships, they must be done to something external to ourselves, namely, the Unknowable.

Religion and Its Function

Sorting out the difference between the "essence and manifestation" of religion is, of course, the particular domain of the phenomenology of religion. Here, we do not intend to venture off down that slippery slope. We are simply suggesting, in light of our explorations into the emergence of the phenomenon of human consciousness, that *the essence of religion is what the human community has decided to do with its experience of awe, wonder, and reverence and the manifestation of that decision constitutes the ingredients of a religious system.*

In order to illustrate the core of our presentation, a comprehensive definition of religion is proposed here, one designed to embrace the range of experiences called "religious" while staying firmly grounded in the world of social reality. Early we discussed religion as embodying the human inclination to muse upon awe, wonder, and reverence, and we suggested that the explaining of the verities of life and probing the Unknown was a preoccupation from early on in our evolution. The storytellers mentioned above held this as their particular domain. So, what we will propose here is a definition of religion which allows for all of it – awe, wonder, reverence, explanations of the verities of life and the Unknown – without ever encroaching upon the issues of ultimate or universal truth. Religion is a genuine human experience and has a specified range of functions. This will, then, constitute our focus and engage our analytical skills.

*Religion is a complex of behaviors and ideologies consisting of rituals and myths which appeals to a **transcendent legitimacy** embodying a worldview* *and ethos addressing the verities of life and existence and conveying a dynamic level of psycho/social reality which is self-validating to the individual and community.*

What we are proposing here is a comprehensive definition of religion, whether prehistoric or contemporary, polytheistic, monotheistic, pantheistic, or non-theistic. Without prejudicing the analysis by setting up superficial tests for truth in some cosmic sense, we are rather stating that religion is a reality of human experience and culture dating from our earliest beginnings and it has functioned in particular ways through the ages. Is it true? Is it real? With that we are not concerned. It is true that religion exists within human experience. It is true that religion is real in that it has been present in every culture and every age from Paleolithic times. In this respect, religion is true, religion is real. However, can we argue here that what religion believes is true – no! Can we argue here that what religion claims to be real is real – no! All we propose to say, and this is saying a lot, is that religion, as a behavioral and ideological form of human activity, exists, has existed from our earliest existence as a human animal, and signs seem to indicate that it will continue to exist in some form in the future.

Now, let us examine each one of these seven components to our comprehensive definition of religion in order that we might test and see that the definition is truly comprehensive and indicative of the phenomenon itself. First, religion is

(1) *a complex of behaviors and ideologies.* Our discussion above regarding ideas and deeds comes in handy here for religion, as a matrix of interactive ideas

and behaviors, embodies the need for the human person and the human community to interface their ideas with action, and, when applied to that which is perceived to be of "ultimate, essential, and fundamental" importance such as religion, ideology and behavior are mutually nurturing. Religion, then, is a "complex of behaviors and ideologies"

(2) *consisting of rituals and myths*. Later we will explore both of these interconnected components in detail but let it suffice here to say that *rituals are the re-enactment of mythic truths* whereas *myths are fantastic stories of epic proportion embodying the fundamental values of an intentional community*. Behaviors and ideologies are, therefore, nurtured and perpetrated by rituals as re-enacted cosmic truths and by myths which carry the essential values of a community. Myths are important in relation to their epic dimensions of value conveyance and rituals are important in relation to their capacity to engage the listener in the re-enacted epic stories of ultimate value. Religion is a complex of behaviors and ideologies consisting of myths and rituals

(3) *which appeals to a transcendent legitimacy*. Herein resides the fundamentally validating ingredient. That is to say, the appeal to the legitimacy of the myths which embody the community's fundamental values and the rituals which are their epic re-enactments rests squarely upon the community's recognition and acknowledgment of their legitimacy in transcendent terms, in terms writ large, in terms of their super worldly, superhuman reality. Myth and ritual are only valid if they embody this level of transcendent legitimacy for only then can those who control the story control those who hear and believe the story. These behaviors and ideologies consist of myths and rituals and appeal to

transcendent legitimacy

(4) ***embodying a worldview and ethos.*** The *worldview consists of the matter-of-fact explanation of the meaning of the world as perceived and experienced by the community and the ethos is the behavioral character embodying the community's value system.* Indeed, human community could not have even come into existence without them. Community cannot exist for long without a worldview and without an ethos. It is the worldview which essentially "explains" the meaning of the world to the community and it is the ethos which embodies the "character" of that believing community. Whether sitting around the camp fire of a Paleolithic cave community or sitting at the feet of the Dalai Lama or the Pope of Rome, the telling of their story is the telling of a worldview, an explanation of the meaning of the world and all things therein. Without a worldview, a community has no core. And where there is a worldview, a view of the meaning of all things, there is an ethos which is the embodiment of the behavior reflective of the meaning of all things as embraced by the believing community. And, furthermore, the worldview and ethos exists for

(5) ***addressing the verities of life and existence.*** A religion which cannot address the verities of life is no religion. By its very nature and function, religion serves to explain the world, what happens, and why, and particularly those things which are otherwise inconceivable, unexplainable, and incomprehensible. Why do bad things happen to good people (?) and why do good things happen to bad people (?) – these are the age old questions which a viable religion answers for a believing community. Whether the storytelling shaman sitting before a Paleolithic campfire or an ancient rabbi standing at the gate of the Kingdom of Judah or a priest

standing at the altar of an urban parish, the giving of answers to the intractable questions of life is what religion does, what it must do if it is to serve the believing community. Never mind that the stories differ from community to community, or age to age, or believer to believer, just so long as the story serves to explain the verities of life thereby "making sense" of what otherwise is a meaningless world of pain, fear, and despair. Religion must do all of this while

(6) *conveying a dynamic level of psycho/social reality*. Religion must not be seen, conveyed, or experienced as unreal, untrue, inauthentic, pretending, or superficially contrived. It must be real – it must be real for the individual and it must be real for the community. It must at all cost be experienced as the authentic thing which it claims to be. Anything less is self-defeating. The problem with a "liberal" religion is that it is too easily discounted for not being portrayed or perceived as seriously real, unique, *sui generis*! Religions fail and fall when they lose their self-validating authenticity. Religion works when it is seen as real. This reality,

(7) *which is self-validating to the individual and community* can stand the test of time so long as each component continues to function. When there is a breakdown in legitimacy – of the behavior and the ideology or the myth and ritual or the capacity to convincingly address the meaning of life or to convey confidence of the explanations offered – religion fails and falls. Religion must be self-validating to both every participating individual and the community as a whole. Anything less brings chaos and confusion, discord and dissention.

Yet, in every age and every clustering of human beings, from the beginning down to the present, there have always been those individuals, perceived by the community and themselves as self-aware, who have as their own personal agenda the compelling inclination to speculate, to hypothesize, to muse about the meaning of life, to query into the standard explanations of religion to the fundamental questions of life and its meaning. It is a tendency most human beings relate to while only a few take up the calling. But this inclination to speculate, the attraction to muse, is a human trait, early on evidenced in artistic expression and burial rituals.

The human animal is more than *Homo sapiens sapiens* ("the wise"), the human animal is likewise *Homo hermeneuticus* ("the interpretor") – one who engages self-consciously in speculative musings, aesthetic expressions, and leisurely cogitations. The notion that there is a simple unilinear progression from magic to religion to philosophy to science is too simplistic, too superficial, too dismissive of the complexity of the human person and the human community. It is not enough to say that magic came and went, religion came and went, philosophy came and went, and science came and stayed! At another time and in another book, we could explore this notion of progression from magic to science through the maturing grids of religion and philosophy, but not here. Others have done it already and well. Let us stay with our own agenda to explore the Paleolithic origins of religious consciousness, a self-reflective awareness of the relatedness of all things offering nurture and comfort in a world fraught with danger and uncertainty.

Burial Of The Dead – A Classic Demonstration

It's all well and good to speak of myth and ritual,

worldview and ethos, ideology and behavior in the abstract, but what is of interest to us here is specificity of application. We haven't marched through a million years of archeological artifacts to give up now. We intend to demonstrate our point by exploring two or three particular illustrations of the function of religious belief, cultural emergence, and political practicality. First, with regard to religious belief and practice, accepting as we expect the reader to do, the elaborate definition of religion just extrapolated, we wish now to explore the ritualistic burial of the dead from the earliest evidence of human reflective consciousness. Reflective self-awareness leads to intentionality of behavior and, as we have argued, behavior grows out of an ideology consisting of world view and ethos resulting in ritual enforced by myth. The earliest instance in Paleolithic times of such a behavioral matrix is evidenced in the ritualistic burial of the dead by Neanderthal peoples. The earliest evidence of ritual interment of the dead in a specifically prepared grave, i.e., demonstrating communal intentionality, is attributed to Neanderthal peoples who often placed flowers and other artifacts within the grave and sprinkled the corpse with ground red earth. These findings, which we will explore in detail in a moment, have resulted in a reassessment of Neanderthal intellectual capabilities, since the evidence suggests the presence of religious beliefs, i.e., speculative musings about life. Proper disposition of the body which is the residence of the human *persona*, the spirit or soul of a person, required both individual speculation about the nature, meaning, and purpose of life, and a communal endeavor of a rather organized, even ritualized, sort.

To date, there is little evidence of material art produced by Neanderthal peoples. On the other hand, two expressions of human feeling do stand out, viz., the ritualistic burial of the dead and the ritualized bear cult. Interment of the dead was an established practice of the Mousterian Neanderthal peoples whose culture was characterized by flake tools found in the site at LeMoustier, Dordogne, in France, and dates from 80,000 to less than 40,000 years ago. Deriving from the Acheulian and perhaps the **Clactonian cultures**, the fossils of *Homo sapiens neanderthalensis* are evidenced prolifically in this location as well as others. A good many of the recovered fossil skeletons of the Neanderthal peoples have been found carefully bedded down in shallow pits and accompanied by flint tools and occasional bones.

One Neanderthal person was buried in the Shanidar Cave in Iran on a bed of pine boughs and flowers, according to the pollen concentrated in the earth surrounding the skeleton. "Whatever this might or might not lead us to infer about belief in immortality and a continued spiritual existence apart from the body," says E. Adamson Hoebel, "it does show concern for the individual as a person." (Hoebel, p. 172.) Even newborn infants were stylistically buried, i.e., in a planned calculated fashion, in the cavern of La Ferrassie in France. The Shanidar site is one of the most elaborated and celebrated of finds in this regard. In the Zagros Mountain highlands of Iraq about 250 miles due north of Baghdad where Kurdish goatherders still live today, is the site about the size of four tennis courts. The site was excavated by Ralph Solecki of Columbia University when he hit bedrock at a depth of 45 feet, which represents deposits up to 100,000 years old. Seven Neanderthal skeletons were found, three of them the remains of people crushed to death by falling rocks. One of the three was apparently recovering from a spear or knife wound in the ribs and at least one of the individuals, a man with a badly crushed skull, was buried deep in the cave with special ceremony. One spring day about 60,000 years ago members of his family or clan went out into the hills, picked masses of wild flowers, and made a bed of them on the ground, a resting place for the deceased. Other flowers were probably laid on top of his grave; still others seem to have been woven together with the branches of a pinelike shrub to form a wreath. Traces of that offering endure in the form of fossil pollen collected from the burial site, the remains of the ancestors of present-day grape hyacinths, bachelor's buttons, hollyhocks, and yellow-flowering groundsels.

These findings, the graves and the patterns around them, mark a great change in human evolution. Death, and presumably life, had become something special. No comparable evidence appears in earlier records, and as far as we know, our ancestors had always died like other animals before Neanderthal times, being abandoned when they were too weak to keep up with the band or wandering off to wait alone for the end to come. Burial implies a new kind of concern for the individual and, according to one theory, it arose as part of a response to bitter glacial conditions when people needed one another even more than in less-demanding times and formed more intimate ties and cared more intensely when death came. Now, when it appears that global warming may mark the beginning of the end for the human community as we now know it, it is ironic that it was glaciation itself that created the geological conditions which fostered human evolution and the appearance of human consciousness.

The evidence of a bear cult among different groups of

Neanderthal peoples is also ample. Bear burials have recently been discovered in the Cavern of Regourdon, in southern France, confirming the importance of the bear-skull cache from the Dragon's Lair (the Drachenloch) in Switzerland, where a stone-lined pit, or cist, held a collection of bear skulls, including the lower jaws. The hole was closed with a large stone slab. The Drachenloch also yielded a bear skull without a lower jaw but with the right thighbone of another bear pushed between the cheekbone (**malar**) and the brain case (**caldarium**) on the right side. This device was found placed upon two shinbones (femurs) from yet two other bears. This level of communal corporate behavioral intentionality is quite remarkable. It leaves little doubt of the refinement in both social communal action and verbal articulation which are unquestionably high as no amount of instinctual behavior could produce such a demonstrable configuration.

Other rituals involving cave bears are in evidence in many archeological sites. Cave bears, of course, had to be driven out of caves before the Neanderthal peoples could inhabit them, and these bears were killed by the hundreds as evidenced by the bone remains. They were, however, respected and appear to be the focus of ritualized veneration before, in actuality, being eaten. A mountain cave in eastern Austria contained a rectangular vault holding seven bear skulls all facing the cave's entrance; while material excavated from Regourdou, another site in southern France, represents perhaps the most elaborate bear-cult burial known. It included a skeleton complete except for the skull (which had probably been taken by an amateur collector), stone drains, a rectangular pit covered by a flat stone slab weighing almost a ton, and the remains of more than twenty cave bears.

Intentionality is, of course, the tell-tell sign of reflective self-awareness, what we are calling here consciousness. "Intentional burial" is a term used, among many scholars, by Robert J. Bradwood (1964:56) and reflects the anthropologist's sense of a concerted corporate action on the part of collaborating individuals. These burials have been found on the floors of the caves (which we will discuss further on) in evidence that the people dug graves in the places where they lived. The holes made for the graves were small and for this reason we think the bodies were placed in a curled-up or "**contracted position**," which was a conventional method of putting the body in the grave, widely found in ancient burials. The body lies curled up on one side as if sleeping. The lower limbs are sometimes markedly flexed, with the knees drawn to the chin to make an angle of 90 degrees or less with the spinal column. The body was probably swathed with **ligatures**, perhaps to keep the spirit from emerging and terrifying the living, but the latter is strictly speculation. Flint or bone tools or pieces of meat seem to have been put in with some of the bodies of the ancients and, in several cases, flat stones had been laid over the graves.

This writer, for one, is much less likely to attribute "spirit fear" to early peoples out of deference to their otherwise logically calculated form of social behavior. In some ways, the present day preoccupation with the corpse of the deceased is no less elaborated than it was a hundred thousand years ago. Today we commonly use the "extended burial" posture in which the body rests on its back in an extended position rather than in some other fashion, but appropriately dressed in our finest as if ready to attend church, synagogue, or the mosque. Other burial options, prehistoric and even sometimes contemporary, include "**flexed burial**," a form of burial in which the arms or legs or both are bent, making the corpse more compact and easier to inter; "**niche burial**," a form of burial in which the body is placed in a niche lateral to the grave shaft; "**olla burial**," a method of interment wherein the body is placed in a large urn and set in a subterranean chamber, practiced among some Native American tribes; and "**platform burial**," a method of disposing of the dead in which the body is placed on a platform above the ground and left to be defleshed by scavengers.

Evidence is prolific, diverse geographically and in presentation form, such that the practice of the ritualistic burial of the dead among Neanderthals is unquestioned by research scholars. John E. Pfeiffer (1969) has explored the subject extensively and here we will pay close attention to his analysis for he exercises great restraint in speculating as to the "reasons why" and rather focuses upon the empirical evidence of the behavior itself. It lies within our purview, however, to speculate upon these hypotheses of ideology and behavior, but our speculation grows out of and is linked to the empirical evidence of ritualized burials themselves. Archeological excavations rarely provide direct information about the feelings of our remote ancestors; usually we are reduced to guesses or otherwise. But now and then the past leaves patterns whose significance cannot be mistaken. During the early 1900's such evidence was uncovered, as we have mentioned earlier, at Le Moustier about thirty miles west of La Chapelle-aux-Saints; it shows that these people had developed a new way of thinking, a new attitude toward life and death, and judging by their behavior we can deduce reflective thought, reasoning, and corporate intentional behavior.

Here, at Le Moustier, a boy of about fifteen or sixteen years old had been buried in a cave. He had been lowered into a trench, placed on his right side with knees slightly drawn and head resting on his forearm in a sleeping position. A pile of flints lay under his head to form a sort of stone pillow, and near his hand was a beautifully worked stone ax. Around the remains were wild-cattle bones, many of them charred, the remnants of roasted meat which may have been provided to serve as sustenance in the world of the dead. (An old man of La Chappelle-aux-Saints was also buried in a trench and surrounded by stone tools.) Not far from the Le Moustier site is a cave which was discovered by a road-building crew and included a set of nine little mounds arranged neatly in three rows. One of the mounds contained the remains of a small infant, perhaps a stillborn infant, and three flint tools. The other eight mounds were empty, but one possibility is that they originally contained food and other supplies for the use of the deceased in the afterlife. This may have been a family cemetery, since the graves of three children and two adults were found near the infant's grave.

Now, of course, we cannot deduce a "theology of life and death" from these empirical remains any more than we could deduce such a theology from excavating a cemetery today. What is evidenced, now and then, is an intentional effort on the part of a community to a ritualized expression of a worldview and ethos endemic to their corporate experience. These instances of burial are too physically demanding and elaborate to be the work of one individual. Therefore, we must conclude that there is a community of consciousness, a belief system in which all participate, which has led to this amount of effort being expended in a exercise not directly related to survival.

Obviously, the empirical remains are rich in symbolism which we cannot decipher. Near Monte Circeo, on the Mediterranean coast between Rome and Naples, is a deep cave whose innermost chamber contained a circle of stones, at the center of the circle a human skull with a hole bored into it. There are also signs that animal rituals were practiced along with burials. A cave in a steep ravine in the mountains of Uzbek in Central Asia held the shallow grave of a young boy, and half a dozen pairs of ibex horns were stuck in the earth around the head end of the grave, suggesting that an **ibex cult** existed here among Neanderthal peoples more than fifty thousand years ago, as it does today among people living in the same region.

Severe climates, speculates Pfeiffer and others, may have had something to do with this new spirit of consciousness. Certainly considerable evidence exists in our own times to suggest that people living under the most depressing circumstances often have the highest hopes for the future, in another world if not in this one. But there had been hard times before, and death must always have been a mysterious phenomenon for, even among the chimpanzees (according to Jane Van Lawick Goodall), there is a worrying and wondering and confusion brought on by the death of a member of the community. The new element was the evolution of a brain capable of framing questions, arriving at answers, and establishing rituals which by the very fact that they were practiced regularly reinforced the validity of the answers (Pfeiffer, p. 171). Ritual expresses the belief or hope that a connection exists between repetition and truth, the notion that if a possibility is stated often enough it becomes a certainty.

Thus, we know that the Neanderthal peoples invented, or at least formalized, illusion when they invented the ritualistic burial of the dead. The belief in an afterlife says in effect that death is not what it seems; that it represents an apparent ending only, an ending only in so far as the evidence of the senses is concerned; and that in this case, the crude evidence of the senses is wrong. Reality involves not observed and observable "facts" but an abstraction, the idea that death is actually a passage from one world to another. This is evidenced by the inclusion of food and hunting equipment and cooking instruments in the graves of the deceased. It is no stretch to surmise what is being imagined by the burying community. Pfeiffer argues that "in this respect the burial ceremonies of prehistoric hunters expressed the kind of thinking used today to develop theories about the structure of the atomic nucleus or the expanding universe."

Chapter Five

Culture
How a Community Lives in the World

We have been suggesting all along that religion is an integral component of our humanness and we have explored empirical evidence of a sense of awe, wonder, and reverence manifested in ritual behavior implying a mythic expressiveness of a worldview and ethos embodied within an intentional community. What we will do here is demonstrate that culture is likewise an integral component of our humanness and the parallels between religion and culture are striking, such that to consider one without the other is irresponsible and counterproductive. Here, we will explore a comprehensive definition of "culture" built upon the foundation set by our definition of religion with only the slightest but crucial difference as relates to legitimacy. Whereas we used the ritualistic burial of the dead as the empirical evidence for religious consciousness among Paleolithic peoples, we will use cave art as the empirical evidence of cultural expressiveness among Paleolithic peoples. But first, let us explore the parameters of our definition of culture.

*Culture is a complex of behaviors and ideologies consisting of rituals and myths which appeals to an **historico-temporal legitimacy** embodying a worldview and ethos addressing the verities of life and existence conveying a dynamic level of psycho/social reality which is self-validating to the individual and community.*

Now, let us examine each one of these seven components of our comprehensive definition of culture in order that we might test and see that the definition is truly comprehensive and indicative of the phenomenon itself. Culture is

(1) *a complex of behaviors and ideologies*. Culture, human culture, is what people do, their actions, their behaviors, that which calls upon intentional engagement and movement, individually and communally. But, as we know, for human beings self-reflectivity and intentionality are predicated upon thought, ideas, notions. People do things for a reason, whether self-consciously intentional or habitually stimulated, whether reasonable or unreasonable. Other than biological instincts, human behavior is motivated by an intention to act, a will to behavior, an awareness of an inclination to respond to an idea, or a thought. Since culture is what people do, it consists of both ideas about doing and the action involved in the doing. But more, ideas which reflect intentionality and lead to behavior invariably include a framework or a pattern of idea/action matrices

(2) *consisting of rituals and myths*. Later we will explore both of these interconnected components in detail but let it suffice here to say that rituals are the re-enactment of mythic truths, whereas myths are fantastic stories of epic proportion embodying the fundamental

behaviors (accomplishments/achievements) of an intentional community. Behaviors and ideologies are, therefore, nurtured and perpetuated by rituals which, by reenacting the accomplishments and achievements of a community, carry the essential values of that community. Myths as stories are valued in relation to their epic dimensions of value conveyance, and rituals are valued in relation to their capacity to engage the listener in the re-enacted epic stories of deeds done well. Culture, then, is a complex of behaviors and ideologies consisting of tales of valued accomplishments and patterned communal activities, i.e., myths and rituals,

(3) *which appeals to an historico-temporal legitimacy*. Herein resides the fundamentally validating ingredient. That is to say, the appeal to the legitimacy of the myths which embody the community's fundamentally valued accomplishments and achievements and the rituals which are their epic re-enactments rests squarely on the community's recognition and acknowledgment of the legitimacy of these myths and rituals in temporal terms, in terms writ large, in terms of their historical reality. Myths and rituals are only valid if they embody this level of real-time (historical/temporal) legitimacy for only then can those who control the story control those who hear and believe the story. In the maturing process of individuals and of communities, the capacity to identify a "true" story from merely a "made-up" story is evidence of growth in self-reflectivity and communal self-consciousness. When children begin to distinguish between the unreality of Santa Claus and the reality of Abraham Lincoln, we say they are "growing up." Historic events, temporally validated activity and achievements, are crucial to the establishment, nurture,

and maintenance of a sense of community, of a sense of communal identity, well-being, and hope for perpetuity. These behaviors, temporally and historically validated, reinforced by their mythic proportions and ritual efficacy for community participation must necessarily appeal to real life legitimacy

(4) *embodying a worldview and ethos.* The worldview consists of the matter-of-fact explanation of the meaning of the world as perceived and experienced by the community, and the ethos is the behavioral character expressive of the community's culture, its deeds, its achievements and accomplishments. Community cannot exist without a worldview or without an ethos. It is the worldview which essentially "explains" the meaning of its achievements to the community and it is the ethos which embodies the "character" of those accomplishments. Whether sitting around the camp fire of a Paleolithic cave community or sitting at the feet of the Dalai Lama or the Pope of Rome, the telling of their story is the telling of a worldview, an explanation of the meaning and purpose of all things done. Without a worldview, a culture has no parameters, no measuring rod of valid behavior, meaningful accomplishment, deeds worth doing for the sake of community. And where there is a worldview, a view of the meaning of all things done, there is an ethos which is the embodiment of the behavior reflective of the meaning of all things accomplished as embraced by the self-validating will of the community. And, furthermore, the worldview and ethos exist for the purpose of

(5) *addressing the verities of life and existence.* A culture which cannot address the verities of life and existence is no culture at all. By its very nature and function, culture serves to validate the community's own

perceived world. The verities of life and existence take on meaning within a self-reflective community aware of and participating in the necessity for deeds, for accomplishments, for achievements, for doing things for the survival, the nurturance, and the maintenance of the community. Culture must do all of this while

(6) *conveying a dynamic level of psycho/social reality*. Culture must not be seen or experienced as unreal, inauthentic, or superficially contrived. It must be real – it must be real for the individual and it must be real for the community. It must at all cost be experienced as the authentic thing which it claims to be. All deeds validated by the community must have worth, value, and purpose, otherwise, the doing of things has no binding force within the community. One can contribute or not, participate or not, be involved or not, and therein lies the danger of culture devolution. Culture as deed, as the doing of what needs to be done, this is the challenge and was the challenge for early peoples as it is for peoples and cultures today. Anything less is self-defeating. Cultures fail and fall when they lose their self-validating authenticity. Culture works when it is seen as real, when there is a corporate ownership of its truly psychological and social reality. This reality,

(7) *which is self-validating to the individual and community*, can stand the test of time just so long as each component continues to function. When there is a breakdown in legitimacy – of the behavior or the ideology or the myth and ritual or the capacity to convincingly address the meaning of life and to convey confidence of the explanations offered – culture fails and falls. Culture must be self-validating to both every participating individual and the community as a whole. Anything less brings chaos and confusion, discord and

dissension.

The human person, prehistoric or contemporary, is more than just *Homo hermeneuticus*, the mandated interpreter of our world, for we are more than just religious. Religious, certainly, according to our definition and the empirical evidence we have brought forth from the ritual burials of our ancestors and the Neanderthal peoples. We are more than just "interpreters" of our environment, we are also socially interactive members of our corporate life. We are **Homo socialis**, for what makes us human is our interactive participation in a community, our sense of heart and hearth, our hunting and gathering activities, our tool-making and artistic endeavors, and our leisure.

Cave Art – A Classic Demonstration

Both religion and art appear in the archeological record with the appearance of *Homo sapiens*, religion with the Neanderthals and art with the Cro-Magnons. The oldest known paintings have been found in association with occupation layers deposited more than 30,000 years ago, at least 40,000 years after the earliest known burial ceremonies. It seems that some forty millennia of evolution were required before descendants of the first "philosophers," the first people to think about death and an afterlife, found reasons to portray things artistically that were important to them.

It seems that art came with a burst on the scene in the sense that from the very beginning the record includes works performed in a mature and established style. A hint of the aesthetic sense or something very close to it is found in early Acheulian times (more later), in occasional hand axes shaped far more beautifully than required for strictly utilitarian purposes. The earliest symbols known from excavations are the stones and ibex horns and cave-bear skulls which the Neanderthals arranged in patterns around the graves of their dead as we have already seen. Personal adornment seems to have been another precursor of art. This involved a new level of assertiveness, a new degree of individuality and personal attention to physical appearance to others. For example, Neanderthal sites commonly include natural pigments, probably to serve as cosmetics for the dead in burial ceremonies as well as for the living, lumps of black manganese and red ocher, some sharpened like pencils and others scratched presumably to make powder.

The Cro-Magnon peoples also used cosmetics and made the earliest known jewelry. They wore clothes decorated with rows of colored beads, ivory bracelets, necklaces of pierced teeth and fish vertebrae. Their more elaborate decorations were related to a general increase in the complexity of communal living, to the rise of more advanced mass-hunting methods, and, therefore, the increased availability of leisure time for artistic expression. It has been suggested that jewelry may have done more than beautify. It may very well have helped to identify the clan or the status of people associating in groups too large for individuals to know one another by sight or name. At the same time, more complex rituals served to teach and sanctify more complex rules of behavior. This is the framework, the social context, in which art had its beginnings. The psychodynamics of personal grooming and adornment is charged with promising insights into the real emergence of class consciousness and a personally driven vanity ego, but here is not the place to pursue what otherwise is a topic of great promise to the paleopsychologist.

The time period we are dealing with here is the Upper Paleolithic, the subdivision of the prehistoric age characterized by a large and refined repertory of **blade tools** and by specialized instruments of ivory and bone. The Upper Paleolithic is dated around 45,000 years ago to about 10,000 years ago. Associated with the advent of early modern *Homo sapiens*, the Upper Paleolithic cultural period saw the increased importance of blade tools, burins or gravers, bone, ivory, and antler tools, and the appearance of a specialized big-game hunting adaptation focusing on reindeer and mammoths. The complexity and diversity of traditions were augmented by art flourishing in many forms from as early as 30,000 years ago to the end of the Upper Paleolithic period. Climaxing particularly in Western Europe, aesthetic expression was found in animal and human figurines; engravings, bas-reliefs, and paintings on rocks, rock shelters, and caves; delicately flaked willow and laurel leaf blades of rainbow flint; carving and incising of bone; and bone necklaces, bracelets, and beads. Art in Europe underwent a decline at the end of the Ice Age, but some see continuity in the animal figurines of the arctic peoples.

Best described from French sites, Upper Paleolithic art is divided into two main types; **art mobilier** (portable art) and **art parietal** (found on permanent surfaces such as cave walls). Portable art includes naturalistic animal figurines of bone, ivory, or fired clay representing antelope, bison, horses, or other large animals. Human "Venus" figurines or females with highly accentuated sexual characteristics – perhaps fertility symbols it has been suggested – were widespread in Europe and are exemplified by the carving from a mammoth tusk from Predmost, Czechoslovakia, the stone Venus of

Willendorf, Austria, and the French ivory figure from Lespugue. (*See illustrative details in Appendix C.*) Carved and perforated bones and teeth were used for personal adornment, and beads were sewn to leather caps and clothing. Flat bone disks, perhaps relics, were perforated and engraved. Bone, ivory, and antler objects were often incised or carved, perhaps as art, status symbols, or for ritual purposes.

Parietal art, the most famous Upper Paleolithic form of aesthetic expression, reaches a climax in the art of the caves and rock shelters of the French Dordogne and Cantabrian Spain at such sites as Lascaux and Altamira. (*See illustrative details in Appendix J.*) Although discovered in 1879, Altamira remained scientifically unaccepted until a number of French finds were also unearthed. Because of the growth of green algae fostered by human presence in the cave, Lascaux is now generally inaccessible to the public. That the really great cave art is pretty well restricted to southern France and Cantabrian (northwestern) Spain we know, but some interesting new groups have been recently found in Russia as well. There are several interesting things about the "Franco-Cantabrian" cave art we should point out before moving on here. It was done deep down in the darkest and most dangerous parts of the caves, although the people lived only in the openings of the caves. Clearly it was the "act of painting" that mattered to these early artists. The artist had to go way down into the most mysterious depths of the cave and create an animal in paint from memory. The cave art of the Franco-Cantabrian style is one of the great artistic achievements of all times. The subjects drawn are almost always the larger animals of that period and, in some of the best examples, the beasts are drawn in full color and the paintings are remarkably alive and charged with energy.

Cave painting occurred during most of the Upper Paleolithic, evolving from simple lines and flat washes to elaborate **polychromes**. Ochre was used for red, yellow, and brown coloring; manganese oxide or charcoal was used for black. These substances were ground into powder and mixed with a lubricant for application. Paintings were often made in inaccessible regions of caves, necessitating the use of lamps. Though game animals, such as bison, horses, deer, and reindeer, were commonly depicted, human figures are scarce and highly stylized by comparison. Human figures often had an animal's head, perhaps representing a shaman or sorcerer it is supposed by art experts. Impressions and outlines of human hands, however, and geometric figures of dots and lines were quite prevalent. Interpretations of cave paintings are numerous and speculative, ranging from the hypothesis that leisure time allowed people to create art for its own sake to the assumption that art for magical and religious purposes was used to increase game animals and ensure hunting success. Although the classic area for defining Upper Paleolithic art is Western Europe, figurines eventually extended as far as Asia. The more refined Australian engravings may date to 18,000 years ago and possibly even earlier.

The world's first great art "movement," says Pfeiffer, lasted more than 20,000 years, from Aurignacian to Magdalenian times. Some of its most spectacular products are found in underground galleries, away from natural light in the passages and chambers and niches of limestone caves, and indicate in a most vivid fashion how completely hunting dominated the attention and imagination of pre-historic peoples. They rarely drew people, and never anything that would be recognized as a landscape, for the overwhelming concern was the game animals seen as individuals, clearly defined and detached, and isolated from their natural settings.

Though it is often difficult to speak of an Upper Paleolithic culture in absolute terms, it is, however, possible to identify cultural clusters and trends leading to a reasonably good categorization of these trends into the Aurignacian, Gravettian, Solutrean, and Magdalenian cultural expressions, all of which were supported by the hunting of large herd animals. The Aurignacian culture dates from about 35,000 years ago in Europe and southwest Asia. The Gravettian culture dates from about 22,000 to 18,000 years ago and is found in Europe and southern Russia. Venus figurines, large breasted, big hipped women possibly depicting pregnancy or fertility, are characteristic of this culture. The Solutrean culture found in Spain and France lasted from about 18,000 to 15,000 years ago. The Magdalenian culture lasted from about 15,000 to 8,000 years ago and was centered in Western Europe, but occurred as far east as Russia. This culture witnessed the invention of the harpoon, the spear-thrower, and **microliths**.

These Upper Paleolithic cultures contain the earliest remains of early people's artistic behavior, including the first known cave paintings which are of special interest to us here. These paintings are almost exclusively of animals as we have said and were often painted one on top of the other, indicating that they may have been of symbolic significance rather than merely artistic expression, though this interpretation is far from universally accepted. As we have said, art as we know it made its first acual appearance among the European Aurignacians. Stylized profile drawings of numerous animals, together with paintings of hands adorn Aurignacian cave walls. The earliest cave paintings in western Europe, including the early ones at Lascaux mentioned earlier, are attributed to this culture.

The Gravettian peoples, ranging from southern Russia to Spain but concentrated in central Europe, were an especially gifted early Upper Paleolithic culture characterized by skilled art. The Gravettians hunted the mammoth and made use of mammoth ivory for tools, weapons, and other implements. They sculpted graceful animal figurines in clay and then fired them. They also carved figurines in bone or ivory, and it was the Gravettians who created the famous "Venus" figurines discussed earlier. Their cave paintings resemble those found in southern France mentioned earlier. Later than the Aurignacian and the Gravettian was the Solutrean, one of the most mysterious industries – and one of the most aesthetic – of the European Upper Paleolithic. The Solutrean lasted a very short time, peaking at about 18,000 years ago. Sites have been found in France, Hungary, Poland, Spain, and southern Russia, and their ancient inhabitants are noted for having produced the finest examples of stone workmanship. The technique of parallel flaking on both faces produced beautiful, highly symmetrical laurel-leaf blades and shouldered points. Unfortunately, however, no human skeletal material has ever been found at any Solutrean site.

The culmination of Upper Paleolithic culture came in France in the Magdalenian period, dating between 15,000 and 10,000 years ago. Magdalenian industries have also been found in Germany, Hungary, and Spain. The outstanding trend during the Magdalenian is the decline of stone tools and their replacement with a variety of bone tools, of which the basic tool form was a harpoon point. The art which had originated during the Aurignacian reached a peak during Magdalenian times. The early animal profiles gave way to distinctive three-dimensional polychrome representations of the animals which these people hunted. Incised work on bone and antler was also spectacular, and the workmanship devoted to these paintings and engravings far exceeds utilitarian needs, thus providing further evidence that aesthetic values were significantly important to Upper Paleolithic peoples.

The great majority of art caves are located in France and Spain, as we have said. According to a recent count, France has sixty-five sites and Spain thirty. About half of all known sites are concentrated in three regions along a ninety-mile stretch of the northern coast of Spain, in the French Pyrenees fifty miles south of Toulouse, and in the countryside around Les Eyzies. No one has answered the obvious question, "Why did such a prolific artistic community among the Upper Paleolithic peoples exist where even today artistic talent and endeavor seem to thrive disproportionately to the rest of Europe and the world?" One need not be a Francophile to be tantalized by the implications of such a question. Not wishing to speculate upon that question, we turn to more practical information. About 120 art caves have been discovered to date, and the list is growing at the rate of about one new cave every year or two. Among recent finds are a cave overlooking the Lot River in southwestern France containing more than seventy engravings, several caves in Italy, and a cave in Brittany which has not yet been fully investigated.

Any attempt to interpret prehistoric art must take account of the fact that artists had more immediate and wider responsibilities in earlier times than they do today.

Human evolution requires learning, teaching, passing ideas on from generation to generation. Today, however, techniques can be written down and passed on with little bother. Pfieffer has pointed out that prehistoric art served a number of purposes, perhaps the least complicated being to bring color and form into the dwelling place of the human community. Most paintings and engravings in living spaces at cave mouths or in rock shelters have disintegrated because they were exposed to the weather, but at other sites, deep inside remote cave tunnels, we find striking examples of elaborated artistic expression which suggests other motives beside or in addition to artistic pleasure may have been at work, such as religious symbolism and even ritual exercises. However, in a recent analysis of cave art, the first really critical analysis recognized by the scholarly community, Peter Ucko and Andrée Rosenfeld of University College of London and the British Museum, respectively, consider it likely that such work "was intended to enliven and brighten domestic activities." And, without putting too fine a point on it, there is something to be said of the unsuppressable "joie de vivre" of the artist as constituting a viable "cause de celebration."

Aptitude, opportunity, and inclination, we have been saying, created the matrix within which human speculation leading to mythic stories and ritualistic re-enactments based upon a worldview and ethos came into existence. Beyond instinct and the sheer demands of survival, peoples of the Paleolithic Age took advantage of the opportunity afforded them by the development of fire-manipulation skills, improved diet and verbal communication, and a substantial upgrade in domicile accommodations to muse and speculate, to ponder and query, and, as we have seen here in our discussion of culture, not only develop communally-validating religious expressions of awe, wonder, and reverence, but also raw and unadulterated artistic expressions as well. Whereas religion appeals to transcendent validation, culture appeals to historical and temporal validation, and no more poignant expression of that validity of life and community exists than the aesthetic sensitivities and expressiveness of a reflectively self-aware people. Whereas religion validated the community by appeals to the "higher powers" enforced by myth and ritual, worldview and ethos, the culture of the people validated the community by appeals to the "here and now" existence expressed in art and craft, sculpture and tool-making. We are who we are by virtue of what we believe and what we do; *our religion reflects our transcendent validation and our culture reflects its historical legitimacy.* When religion dissipates, the transcendently-validating worldview and ethos decline; and, when religion is in decline, the historical and temporal validity of a people sees the culture fall into shambles as well.

In each subsequent cultural shift from the Aurignacians to the Magdalenians to the Solutreans, to the **Gellitians**, there was a shift in the physical world brought on by a changing climate and a concurrent shift in artistic expression brought about by a shifting worldview. Both religion and culture survive and thrive when they nurture each other; when one declines, the other inevitably does likewise. But when religion and culture are in harmony, when they compliment each other, when they shore each other up with a transcendent and historically validating view of the world and the community's rightful place in it, then we see the emergence of politics, of the *Homo politicus* of the human animal who is bound to seek to control, manipulate, dominate, cooperate, and nurture in order to survive.

Chapter Six

Politics
Confluence of Religion and Culture for Power and Control

From *Homo hermeneuticus* (religious man) to *Homo socialis* (social man) to *Homo politicus* (political man), the human person and the human community have evolved by virtue of the complimentary of these fundamentally human characteristics – a desire to interpret the world, to relate to one's peers, and to control that world and those peers for the survival of the whole community. From the outset, we have been suggesting that religious consciousness is the human capacity to be self-aware and reflectively intentional about the personal experience of awe, wonder, and reverence in the world and a desire to systematically express that experience corporately. Furthermore, we have suggested that religion is complimented by culture in that, whereas religion appeals to a transcendent legitimacy, culture appeals to an historical and temporal legitimacy. Both, we have illustrated, are made up of a complex of behaviors and ideologies consisting of rituals (re-enactments of value-charged saga stories) and myths (those value-charged saga stories ritualistically expressive of the community's self-understanding) which appeals to both a transcendent and an historical legitimacy embodied in a worldview (the world as it really is) and ethos (a people's behavioral character informed by the real world) addressing the uncertainties of life conveyed in a psychological and social reality that is unquestionably validating to both the individual and the community.

When defined in this way, we suggest that no human community can exist without both religion and culture. And yet, something is missing, that sense beyond meaning and purpose of an individual's life and the community's life, which brings order to the community, which brings a sense of patterned existence depended upon by everyone and called upon when uncertainty and confusion emerge within the social body. What is missing is a mechanism, self-validated, for control, for order, for pattern, for system, for process. Without this mechanism, religion and culture lose their way, fail to focus, cease to provide a view of the present and a hope for the future. Without the management of power, without control, without the mechanism for dominance, manipulation, and cooperation, survival is not possible, nurturance falls by the wayside. Where two or three are gathered together, someone must be in charge!

Politics is a complex of behaviors and ideologies consisting of rituals and myths which appeal to a confluence of transcendent and historico-temporal legitimacy embodying a worldview and ethos addressing the verities of life and existence conveying a dynamic level of psycho/social reality which is self-validating to the individual and community.

Homo Politicus does not simply imply a governmental framework and mechanism. Rather "Political Man" is a characteristic of all human persons and communities wherein there is the existence of an operational system of authority and power, control and dominance, designed ostensibly for the survival of the group. So in every expression of social life, whether familial, religious, or artistic, all such behavior is based upon an ideological mutuality of understanding delegating the right or asserting the right to control, to govern, to interpret, to nurture. And this willingness or readiness to acknowledge the role of leadership within the community is an integral component of our survival history. Therefore, we have, as will be seen here, attempted to define politics in the same manner as we have defined religion and culture. It is left to the argument and to the reader to determine whether our attempt has been successful.

As before with religion and culture, let us examine each component of our proposed definition of "politics" to see how it might work in this overall system of analysis relative to our quest for the Paleolithic origins of religious consciousness.

(1) *Politics is a complex of behaviors and ideologies* by which we mean that in the daily activities of the human community there is a constellation of ideas, notions, perceptions, suspicions, and attitudes which give rise to a corporate response to every situation arising within the community. Relationships, whether dyadic, triadic, or multi-componential, suggest and exemplify the presence of dominance, authority, and deference. Whether it affects the relationship between just two people or the relationship within the broader context of the whole community, such behavioral posturing as deference to power brought on by

the unchallenged exercise of authority is inevitable. The *persona* of leadership, the conveyance of dominant ability and skill, the determination of control by one or a few over two or more members of a community are evidence of politics. And, whether this *persona* is for personal gain or community well-being, there is the implied notion that it is all approved in relationship to the necessity of survival. An individual and a community will delegate or relinquish the exercise of power and control to anyone or any group who can offer assurance of survival. As in religion and culture, political ideologies and behaviors inevitably emerge as

(2) *consisting of rituals and myths* for, as with religion and culture, ideas and action all feed off of and are fed by the rituals of a community and the myths which nurture them. The mythic stories which keep a community focused upon its own survival center around "success" of endurance, its accomplishments, its achievements, events of epic proportion which must be told again and again. Ritual is the re-enactment of these epic stories of survival and achievement. Even today, in the United States, we relive the communal past on the 4th of July, on Memorial Day, even, though politically incorrect these days, Columbus Day. These reenactments of the great mythic sagas which define who we are date from our earliest existence. Ideas and their precipitating behavior are fed and nurtured by these mythic tales and their communal reenactments

(3) *which appeal to a confluence of transcendent and historico-temporal legitimacy,* for these myths

are not just recounted historical events, as important as temporal history is to a community's self-understanding, but they appeal to a higher power, a greater good of communal value. They represent the highest good, the highest ambition, the greatest of accomplishments, these mythic tales and sagas which are reenacted ritually in communal festivities. Politics, like religion and culture, feeds off these stories and trusts in their value owing to the source of their power which is in and through history yet higher than history. They, indeed, have transcendent roots and transcendent value, for in them there is the embodiment of

(4) *a worldview and ethos* which casts the stories and rituals, legitimated in the ideas and behaviors of a community, into both historical and transcendent perspective. The worldview of any community consists of the matter-of-fact explanation of the meaning of the world which allows for, permits, even encourages the exercise of power and control by those validated by that community to wield such authority. Likewise, the ethos of that community embraces the character of compliance and obedience necessary for its survival. This willingness to delegate authority and to respond to it occurs within every community which survives. It is the worldview and ethos which are seen by all as fundamentally

(5) *addressing the verities of life and existence* confronting every community in every time and place. The Neanderthals, the Cro-Magnons, and all early Paleolithic peoples both welcomed and perpetuated the *Homo politicus* as an inevitability

of survival. With no exercise of authority, with no demonstration of leadership in wielding power and control over the community, with no dominance among the strongest or most persuasive, then there would be no survival. The relinquishing of one's own personal rights and desires in deference to the delegation of the establishment, maintenance, and application of those rights and privileges to recognized leadership was necessary for the survival of the whole community. Therefore, in the interest of communal well-being, nurturance, and survival, early peoples ushered in a political mechanism which they themselves validated. This delegating of control, the implementation of a political machine, was possible because it was seen by the community as

(6) *conveying a dynamic level of psycho/social reality*. The putting into place of a leadership mechanism, a system of rule by the one or the many, was experienced and then expressly validated by ritual and myth, worldview and ethos, such that the system, whatever it proved to be, was understood by the individual and the community as reflective of what was seen and thought to be real; it embodied the social reality of life psychologically and socially. To question the leadership model, the mechanism of control and the exercise of authority, was to question the very infrastructure of an intentional community. Such questions would destroy the fabric of society because the reality of the system needed for survival had been demonstrably proven real and true and universally efficacious through the

telling of the mythic sagas reenacted by communal rituals, verifying that they represent the greatest good for the greatest number of the community, approved by time and history as well as by the transcendent

(7) *which is self-validating to the individual and community.* The whole religious, cultural, and political system exists to self-validate each person and the entire community. Nothing less will do.

It is our contention here that the confluence of religion and culture is most poignantly demonstrated in the emergence of politics. Religion and culture converge as meaning-systems upon the community's capacity to survive. Politics makes that survival possible. Survival is ultimately the driving force of all social life and religion (as an interpretational mechanism) and culture (as an historically expressive mechanism) converge and coagulate within the community seeking out and validating the exercise of authority over itself. This relinquishing and delegating characteristic of the human animal is essential to its survival. Not everyone can lead, not everyone can be in control, for not everyone embodies the gifts of leadership, the inclination to domination, the drive to nurture, and the determination to survive. Only the few, only the chosen, only the designated ones within a gathering of human beings can embrace and exercise such leadership.

Agriculture – A Classic Demonstration

We have been suggesting that complementing the religious and cultural sensibilities of the Paleolithic peoples is their drift, indeed, plunge towards a political structure in the exercise of authority needed for the survival of the community. Nothing short of control, governance, and leadership would do. And, quite clearly, the community, clan, tribe, or multi-family gathering would have looked for leadership to those individuals within their own ranks who had demonstrated skills in this area. Because of the reliance upon the hunt as the mechanism for providing a sustained supply of needed protein, the hunt and all that goes with it was certainly where the community looked for such leadership. The hunt is not merely an adventurous event producing meat for communal consumption. Certainly, this was the initial and obvious outcome but the hunt constituted a phenomenal complex of converging factors making it the single most important shared event within the human matrix of collaboration.

Food and **horticultural wisdom**, language development, and leadership and organizational skills all derive from the communal experience of the hunt. We will argue in a moment that it was within the context of agriculture that the human animal became quite decidedly a "political being," or *Homo politicus*. And, though we believe we make the case effectively, we must commence the argument by addressing the dynamics of the hunt and the ingredients making the hunt successful and, thus, contributing fundamentally to the survival of the human species. Of the three major contributions to the politicization of the human corporate experience, which are (1) food and horticultural wisdom, (2) language development, and (3) leadership and organizational skills, we suggest that the major contribution of women was to the former (1) and men to the latter (3) with both contributing more or less equally with the middle one (2).

We argue for the primacy of women in food and horticultural wisdom (knowledge of medicinal herbs and cooking species as well as being able confidently and consistently to identify edible roots, nuts, plants, fruit, etc.) owing to the physical necessity of their staying close to camp – keeping the fire always going, minding the young as well as the elderly, and foraging for food stuffs such as roots, nuts, plants, fruits, and long term preparations involved in cooking, garment making and garment repairing. Less exciting than the hunt, tending the "home fires" and all that was implied in that was crucial to the corporate survival of the clan. Women (and girls as learners), of necessity, did this work and, we can be assured, were deeply valued for doing it for, indeed, knowing about food preparation, garment making and repairing, medicinal herbs and food spices, etc., could not have gone unnoticed nor undervalued by people living on the very cusp of extinction.

On the other hand, the hunt was the domain of men (and boys as learners). Anthropologists suggest that in traditional hunting societies today, only about 20 - 30% of the food nutrients available in the community are actually provided by means of the hunt (the lion's share coming from the foraging of the women), yet the value of the protein gained from the hunting of large game by Neanderthal and Cro-Magnon men was crucial. Besides the obvious value of the animal protein from the hunt, there were the skins, antlers, hooves, bones, etc., which were also used for the betterment of the clan. Nothing was wasted. It was in the planning and execution of the hunt itself where key leadership and organizational skills came to the fore in the interpersonal relations of the hunting party – youthful trainees, seasoned hunters, and old veterans. The cognitive skills needed to remember past experiences, draw from that memory, plan a future event, arrange the duties and responsibilities of the various hunting party members, leading and directing the hunt itself, executing the killing of the beasts, and, finally, the butchering and distributing of the kill, all presumed the presence of a duly recognized leader and organizer. Even today such a big hunt could not occur without significant planning, allocating of responsibilities, and execution skills in carrying it out. Certainly, the development of reflective thought, intentionality of purpose, and cognizance of consequences all suggest a refined and well-conceived plan requiring a thoughtful human effort.

And, whereas women were tending the home fires (and all that that implies) and men were bringing home the bacon (and all that that implies), life within the gathered community around the fire and over the meal was itself fertile ground for the continued refinement of linguistic acuity. Neurological refinements of the brain, biological refinements of the throat, mouth, and tongue, social opportunity in interpersonal interaction, and emotional predisposition to communicate were all necessary for the development of human speech. Much speculation and little resolution has taken place regarding why other mammals have not developed speech and, though there is much to discuss about that matter, there is little at this point to decide. Let it suffice our argument here to say merely that these ingredients – (1) refined brain and tongue, (2) opportunity, and (3) predisposition to communicate, all contributed to the fundamentally dominant human characteristic, namely, audible, comprehensible speech. (*See illustrative details in Appendix O.*)

We are suggesting, then, that the convergence of social life within the cave, around the fire, over the enjoyment of food, would have provided the most natural and ready-made laboratory for speech development. That is, women and girls sharing their stories of the day's activities with observations about the food and the family and the environs of cave life, and men and boys sharing their stories about the hunt, its planning and execution, and any asides which might spice up an interesting story for group sharing. Here, again, we believe that though all would more or less participate in these stories according to their maturity and language acuity, there would be one or a few, both men and women, who would have naturally excelled in the telling of the stories. And, in the telling of stories lies the power for the telling. Here, as we have suggested earlier, would have been the fertile ground for the development and nurture of the medicine woman and the priest. It is they who embodied the power of the group by controlling the stories of the group, those stories that fed the myths which produced the rituals, built upon and nurturing a worldview of meaning and an ethos of activity based upon what the group believed to be really true about the world in which they lived. One would argue persuasively that doctors and clergy still today wield an inordinate portion of power and authority over communities due to the "mystery" of their respective professional crafts.

The evolution from hunting to **hunting and gathering** and then to slashing and burning and finally to agriculture is a fascinating story of the rise of *Homo politicus*. Whereas religion evolved as a means of dealing with the meaning of life and culture appeared as the expression of social relationships, politics is linked more pragmatically and specifically to survival for, as we have pointed out, food and shelter were directly involved in the process. The Neanderthals were successful in their quest for safe, warm domiciles during the Paleolithic period. It took *Homo sapiens* in the Neolithic period to elevate food-getting to an agricultural industry. But, before agriculture, before **slash and burn** food getting techniques, before the art and skill of gathering so characteristic of Neanderthal and Cro-Magnon peoples, the hunt itself was fundamental. The line is direct and clearly marked from hunting to farming and the story is fascinating because the shifting in food substances and food preparation had a direct inpact upon the biological improvements of early humans and the concomitant social relationships related to food getting.

Hunter and Whitten (*Encyclopedia of Anthropology*:1976) have provided a splendid synopsis of the nature of hunting in its early manifestations and the long range implications of the developing art of food getting. Hunting, they point out, is much more than a means of procuring meat and other valued animal products. Hunting furnishes a unique set of social, psychological, and intellectual rewards, and its impact on myth, ritual, and social relations often transcends its economic importance. We have already explored somewhat the role of hunting as more than just providing protein sources for the clan's survival while inhabiting the caves of southern France and elsewhere. The hunt, fundamentally, became a generator of mythic sagas of great adventure and heroic feats of courage and dedication and, indeed, sacrifice for the community. Such stories, generated by the raw experience of the great hunt, fed the need for the early communities to bond together, to establish identity, foster mutuality of concern and loyalty. Certainly the hunt provided sumptuous dining on high protein sources such as saber tooth tigers, cave bears, and most commonly the mammoth. And, not to be forgotten, great sources of clothing from the pelts and tools from the bones as well as jewelry from the teeth and claws from the hunt. Yes, the hunt and the resulting social activity greatly nurtured the communal sense of identity, serving religion by providing a rationale for survival as determined by the transcendent powers that rule the world, while simultaneously serving culture by providing a demonstration of the historical value of the community. Finally and most definitely, the hunt served the community by demonstrating the indispensability of the management of power and control, the evidential centering of authority within and over the community exercised by the leaders of the hunt and the teller of their tales of courage and achievement.

However, it was actually during the late Paleolithic period when early *Homo sapiens* began seriously to develop alternatives to hunting and gathering as a means to survival. William A. Haviland of the University of Vermont (*Anthropology*: 1974) has provided one of the most lucid explications of the process of any modern anthropologist and we will draw extensively from his analysis though modified to our own particular interest here. In the Late Paleolithic, people were engaged in hunting, fishing, and gathering whatever the environment was kind enough to provide. There is little or no evidence in Paleolithic remains to indicate that livestock was domesticated or that grain was cultivated. Paleolithic peoples did, however, follow the wild herds of reindeer and buffalo and other range animals but the technical knowledge for the care and maintenance of domesticated animals or replantable seeds was still quite evidently absent.

It was the **Neolithic** (New Stone Age) which saw the major transition from foraging for food to the domestication of animals and the cultivation of plants. Though the Neolithic extends beyond the overall intent of our exploration of the Paleolithic origins of religious consciousness, it might serve as a closing point to our study to say a few words about the rise of agriculture as the matrix within which politics as a full blown enterprise of early peoples became evident. The transition from the Paleolithic to the Mesolithic period (about 12,000 years ago) was gradual and was related to the geological changes occurring in Europe due to major climatic conditions. The development by **Mesolithic** peoples of microliths provided them with an important advantage not found in the Upper Paleolithic tools: the small size of the microlith enabled people to devise composite tools made out of stone and wood or bone. Thus, people could make sickles, harpoons, arrows, and daggers by fitting microliths into grooves in wood or bone handles. This refinement of tools greatly advanced the transition from hunting to agriculture. (*See illustrative details in Appendix H.*)

The process of cultivation among Mesolithic-Neolithic cultures (9,000 to 11,000 years ago) did not begin with sowing. And not insignificantly, owing to major climatic changes, the shifting of the cradle of human cultural and communal development was from southern Europe to the Fertile Crescent. Early forms of food production preceded the actual growing of crops and the **domestication** of animals. For example, acorns were bleached to remove the tannin thereby making them edible. Gourds were hung up to be used as hives for bees.

We know, for instance, that prior to attempts by Neolithic peoples to engage in cultivation, early humans would have been careful observers of natural phenomena for they had learned to be environmentally observant during their thousands of years of hunting and gathering. The wisdom needed to survive not only proved enduringly helpful but the skill in natural observation was certainly heightened as well. We are fully aware that early peoples had to be extremely ingenious in order to acquire enough food to satisfy their needs through the long winters. Hunting wasn't enough; they needed sustainable and predictable sources of food beyond meat. Agriculture was an inevitability for early peoples to ensure their survival. The knowledge and skill of interpreting environmental change coupled with a sense of authority which comes with survival wisdom would have certainly elevated some individuals among others within the gathered community.

Analysis of plant and animal remains at a site will usually indicate whether or not its occupants were food producers. A botanist can often tell the fossil of a wild plant species from a domesticated one by a study of the husk and of the stem that holds the seed of the plant. For example, wild cereal grasses, such as barley, wheat, and corn, have a very fragile stem, whereas domesticated cereals have a tough stem. The structural change from a soft to a tough stem in early cultivated plants was probably an unintentional result of selection. When the wild grain stalks were harvested, their soft stems would shatter at the touch of a sickle or flail, and their seeds would be lost. It seems probable then that seeds harvested would be taken from the tough plants. Early domesticators probably also selected seeds from plants having few husks or none at all – eventually breeding them out – because husking prior to pounding the grains into meal or flour was much too time consuming.

The consequences of **cultivation** and domestication are so momentous for the development of civilization that their origin should be examined carefully. Several theories have been proposed to account for this change in the subsistence pattern of early peoples. One major theory is the "oasis" or "desiccation" theory, based on climatic determinism. Its proponents have advanced the idea that the glacial cover over Europe and Asia caused a southern shift in the rain patterns from Europe to northern Africa and southwest Asia. When the glaciers retreated northward, so did the rain patterns. Drying resulted in northern Africa and southwest Asia, and people were forced to congregate at oases for water; because of the scarcity of wild animals in such an arid environment, early peoples were driven by necessity to collect the wild grasses and seeds growing around the oases. Eventually people had to cultivate the grasses to provide enough food for the community. According to this theory, domestication began because the oases attracted hungry animals, such as wild goats, sheep, and also cattle, which came to graze on the stubble of the grain fields, thereby naturally fattening themselves up for human consumption.

There is little empirical evidence to substantiate such a theory. Pollen analysis, for example, has failed to show evidence of a drastic climatic change. The theory does not explain why plant and animal domestication occurred in areas that did not dry out, such as tropical southeast Asia or South America. And it does not explain why, during droughts, sheep and goats would migrate to low-lying oases rather than to the wetter hills. So, another theory proposes that the earliest farming villages were located in the foothill regions of southwest Asia, rather than in the oases and floodplains. We will argue later that the human tendency to allocate and delegate the exercise of authority on behalf of and over a community grows out of the agricultural necessity of claiming land which then has to be held against outsiders. The proponents of this alternative theory regarding farming villages in southeast Asia and South America believe that domestication originated in areas in which the wild counterparts of the early domesticates are found in abundance. In southwest Asia, these zones were found in the hilly regions of the Fertile Crescent, the region formed by the confluence of the Tigris and Euphrates rivers, where large herds of wild goats and sheep and large stands of wild wheat and barley could be found. After people had familiarized themselves with their environment and settled down in one area, they began to domesticate the plants and animals they had previously gathered. This theory, then, proposes a cultural rather than an environmental explanation.

Permanent settlements were an important result of Neolithic domestication and cultivation, whatever their origin. Although there are some exceptions, evidence of sedentary communal life does provide clues as to the connection between people's "settling down" and their early agricultural accomplishments. And, if farming was on its way, villages and towns could not be far behind. Robert M. Adams has said, "The rise of cities, the second great revolution in human culture (following agriculture), was pre-eminently a social process, an expression more of changes in man's interaction with his fellows than in his interaction with his environment" ("The Origin of Cities, *Scientific America*, Vol. 203,2060: 153). Permanent settlements were an important result of

Neolithic domestication and cultivation. There was a gradual transition among tribes from the nomadic to the sedentary way of life. In favored localities, such as the lowlands of Mesopotamia, villages grew into towns, and, in some cases, into cities. The first cities appeared in the fertile river valleys of Mesopotamia, India, and Egypt. With urbanization, a new way of life developed, population increased, writing developed, trade intensified, and new inventions, such as the wheel, drastically changed the technology of Neolithic peoples.

When all of these characteristics coalesced – innovations in farm technology, growth of specialized skills, and the emergence of social classes – there was a growing need for strong organization and control. Nowhere could this be more in evidence than the correlation between farming and land ownership which gave rise to the need for government which would both sort out disputes within a community and serve as a protection against outside intervention. It is a small step from agriculture to the military industrial complex and the role of the political confluence of religion and culture becomes self-evident.

Conclusion

Our intent has been bold here, namely, to demonstrate that religious consciousness emerged in consort with the evolution of the human animal as a natural expression of our awareness of and capacity to respond to a sense of awe, wonder, and reverence in the world. That the human animal in the Paleolithic Age developed sufficiently in terms of biological capacity, sociological opportunity, and psychological inclination to evolve a self-reflective sensibility has been demonstrated by our exploration of the rise of religion, culture, and politics. This tripartite human construct constituted the matrix within which and out of which religious consciousness emerged.

The sense of a transcendent legitimacy (religion) fostered by an historically validated reality (culture) converging within the caldron of power-brokering and influence-pedaling complexification (politics) is what leads us to think of the human animal in terms separate from other members of the primate world. The Paleolithic origins of religious consciousness have been demonstrated here and this insight validates the current interest in religious systems and religious behaviors. Systems and behaviors, as we have seen, both unite and separate the human animal within our own self-understanding. The fact that wars can be waged over the viability of a religious worldview is sufficient to validate the study of it. If we have done nothing else, we have demonstrated the fundamental role of religion in the emergence of the human animal as a species and human society as a world phenomenon.

Not once have we embarked upon that slippery and precarious slope of the pursuit of religious truth nor have we dared speak of God. We have stayed firmly planted on *terra firma*. We have focused upon sociological, psychological, and biological dimensions of human experience. We have purposefully left speculations regarding philosophical and theological hypotheses to the sidelines, preferring to focus upon scientifically demonstrable phenomena in the world of human behavior. Leaving speculative musings to the armchair anthropologists and metaphysicians, we have chosen to focus upon scientifically evidential demonstrations of animal behavior, conditioned by the physical capabilities of the animal in question, our social life, and our emotional inclinations.

By leaving the theologians to their own non-empirical devices of speculation and dogma, our effort has been to explicate the meaning of artifacts left by our Paleolithic ancestors using scientifically current understandings of the human person's physical, social, and psychological makeup. Rather than commencing with a book of rules, a received text of sacred sayings, an extraneous revelation appearing magically or mysteriously in textual or trans-human media, we have rather gone to the caves, the archeological digs, the prehistoric arenas of human activity to find empirical demonstrations of human inclinations regarding our encounter with and our attempts to describe and explain the verities of life. A discussion of the origins of religious consciousness from a philosophical or theological perspective constitutes quite a different agenda for these perspectives commence with dogma and ideology whereas we have commenced

Conclusion

with empirical data gleaned from the archeological findings of modern science. With archeological paraphernalia lying before us on the ground and in the caves, we have rather chosen to examine the evidence of human behavior interpreted through a scientific grid of empirical analysis.

With this we bring our discussion to a close, having proposed a phenomenological explanation as to the origins of religious consciousness based upon archeological data and behavior analysis rather than a transcendent explanation based upon creeds of faith and ideological systems of theological speculation. Religious consciousness, mediated through culture and politics, did, indeed, emerge in the early dawn of Paleolithic times and is, to be sure, ever present with us today. Whether the human animal will continue to hold firmly to the experience of awe, wonder, and reverence for the world in which we live without likewise clutching the ideological baggage which systems of transcendental speculation insist upon carrying is a question yet to be answered. It is possible, just possible, that the human animal's fascination with the mysteries of the world in which we live might one day allow us to extricate ourselves from the faith-based trappings of an intervening transcendence and replace it with a genuine appreciation for the intrinsic beauty and grandeur of the universe itself devoid of an outside validating power. We shall see.

Glossary

Arboreal environment An environment dominated by trees. The kind of environment from which pre-human primates and eventually hominoids evolved before moving to the savannas.

Acheulian Culture A tool-making culture of *Homo erectus* (see elsewhere) in which the Chellean handax was further perfected and finished. The time period was the lower Paleolithic age in the Old World, lasting from the early second interglacial period until the third interglacial period. The name derives from a site at Saint-Acheuil, France. The Acheulian hand axes were smaller and better made than those of the Chellean culture. Many open-air sites date from this period. There was evidence of aesthetic interest in the technology, and the tools were more symmetrical, with sharper edges indicating not just an interest in efficiency but also in beauty. Indirect percussion may have been used from 100,000 to 180,000 years ago. Acheulian culture spread from France and Spain to southern England, southwestern France, and Italy, ultimately overlapping with the eastern culture along the Rhine.

Agnosticism The theory of knowledge which asserts that it is impossible for an individual to attain knowledge of a certain subject-matter, or, more pointedly, the belief that it is impossible to know whether there is a God or a future life, or anything beyond material phenomena. The word was invented by Thomas Henry Huxley, the grandfather of Sir Julian Huxley, who was called "Darwin's bulldog" because of his aggressive support of Darwin's theory of evolution.

Alexeev, Valery Pavlovich Dr. Alexeev received his doctorate from the Institute of Ethnography at the Academy of Sciences in Moscow. He was a scholar at the Institute of Oriental Languages and at the Institute of Ethnography. For some years he directed the Institute of Archaeology in Moscow.

Anthropomorphism The ascription of human characteristics to objects that are not human, found in many early religious beliefs. Modern religions such as Christianity, Judaism, and Islam attribute human characteristics and traits to their god which is a form of anthropomorphism, such as attributing "anger," "jealousy," "love," etc., to god.

Artifact An object of any type made by human hands and by intentional effort. Tools, weapons, pottery, and sculptured and engraved objects are representative artifacts as well as cave paintings, domiciles, and altered environments made suitable for ritual acts.

Aurignacian Culture Refers to the original Upper Paleolithic culture of the Old World, between the Mousterian and Solutrean levels. Bone artifacts, varied flint tools, careful burials, art objects, and ornamentation characterize this culture. The Aurignacian dates back some 40,000 years to about 28,000 years ago. The Cro-Magnons are associated with this period which was marked by the Würm recession (which see). Implements and red ocher used by the person while alive were buried with him along with jewelry. Flint points were used to make the bone artifacts. Some of the bone, horn, and ivory tools were treated by rubbing and sawing. The representative style of art was three dimensional. Graphic art works were executed and bas-reliefs of persons and animals were made as mural decorations. Figurines of women were made from lumps of limestone and Aurignacian caves often have animals modeled in clay and profile engravings of game animals. Dress and adornment were used. The Aurignacians probably began their culture in Asia and went to Europe, where their better social organization enabled them to displace the Mousterian peoples rather abruptly. Aurignacians were tall and well muscled and had a considerable cranial capacity. Their big leap forward is the production of blade tools by flaking pieces of stone off a larger piece of stone, thought to be an indication of more refined tool making skills and excellent examples of their work have been found in such famous sites as St. Cessaire and Chauvet Cave in France and the L'Arbreda Cave in Spain.

Australopithecus africanus A genus of fossil hominoid first found at Taung in South Africa that is dated from the Lower Pleistocene age. The Australopithecinae include a considerable variety of near human and human forms, ranging from pygmies to giants. The Taungs baby, a child's skull which was the first of several dozen individuals from the same area, had a thick skull and a brain which was much smaller than modern man's. The manner in which the head is set on the spine and the shape and position of the pelvic bone indicate that this creature walked erect. The teeth indicate that the jaw was hinged in a human way and that food chewing was rotary rather than up and down like an ape's. There are two genera, the Parenthropus and the Plesianthropus. It is difficult to date these finds, but the animals found with them indicate that they are probably early Pleistocene or late Pliocene, so the Australopithecinae may be up to one million years old. The brain had a volume of around 600 cc. and the jaws were large and projecting. The nuchal crest is low and the molars large. The brain case, supraorbital ridges, and forehead have more human than ape characteristics, as do the cheekbone, jaws, and the joint between lower jaw and skull base.

Azilian A transitional culture area of the Epipaleolithic Age in France. It is named after a site at Mas d'Azil, France. The Azilian remains were found above a Magdalenian and under a Neolithic deposit. This culture is not so refined as the Magdalenian. Round scrapers and points were typical. Fairly crude flat stag antler harpoons were found. Representational art no longer exists, and the culture seems meager. It centered in the Pyrenees region but spread to Switzerland, Belgium, and Scotland. The climate was arboreal but approached modern climate.

Behavior Human action particularly as relates to intentionality and self-awareness.

Biogenesis Suggests the evolutionary processes of biological development.

Biomorphic art The type of designs on small stones made by humans of the Paleolithic Age. The designs were based on organic forms such as animals.

Blade tools A parallel-sided narrow, long flint flake, fairly flat and thin, and often fairly large which emerged early among ancestors of *Homo sapiens sapiens* during the Paleolithic period of human evolution. Its refinement continued to reflect the increasing dexterity and sophistication of emerging human crafts.

Brow ridge The bone structure above the eyes running across the forehead. The brow ridge was pronounced among prehistoric humans and even more so among modern apes but with the evolution of the human animal the brow ridge thinned and receded allowing for the eyes to be more exposed and function better with the complementing bipedalism. In turn, the forehead of the human animal became pronouncedly vertical whereas with the great apes it has remained somewhat horizontal with a pronounced brow ridge sheltering the eyes.

Bulbs of percussion A lump or mass at the end of a flake disengaged from a flint by a hammer blow.

Burial position The presentation of the corpse by an intentional community.

Burial position (Contracted) A conventional method of putting the body in the grave widely found in ancient burials. The body lies curled up on one side as if sleeping. The lower limbs are sometimes markedly flexed, with the knees drawn to the chin to make an angle of 90 degrees or less with the spinal column. The body was probably swathed with **ligatures**, perhaps to keep the spirit from emerging and tarrying among the living (but this, of course, is strictly speculative).

Burial position (Extended) Burial in which the body rests on its back in an extended position, most commonly used in modern times in the West.

Burial position (Flexed) A form of burial in which the arms or legs or both are bent, making the corpse more compact and easier to inter.

Burial position (Niche) A form of burial in which the body is placed in a niche lateral to the grave shaft. It is found in many parts of the world, especially in traditional societies.

Burial position (Olla) A method of interment wherein the body is placed in a large urn and set in a subterranean chamber, practiced by the Zapotec Indians. Excavations at the Tres Zapotes site in the early 1940s unearthed five complete ollas.

Burial position (Platform) A method of disposing of the dead in which the body is placed on a platform above the ground and left to be defleshed by scavengers.

Caldarium A bathing room in Ancient Rome.

Cave painting (art parietal) Painting on cave walls, especially those done during the European Paleolithic period. Parietal art is distinguished from *art mobilier*, which comprises paintings that are movable.

Châtelperronian Period The Châtelperronian period is the name given to similar Upper Paleolithic Neanderthal stone tool assemblages, from about 32,000 to 30,000 years ago. Mostly the tools were made from stone flakes, thin, sharp pieces of flint. If this is indeed a stone tool kit produced by Neanderthals, it is one of the very few known.

Chellean handax More sophisticated all-purpose cutting tool developed from the Olduwan chopper; dates from about one million years ago.

Chellean Culture A Paleolithic culture that lasted from the first glacial period (see elsewhere) through the second interglacial period. The type site was at Chelles, France, and the basic tool was a large core implement serving as a crude hand ax. Core implements originated in this culture and probably were produced around 600,00 years ago in Egypt and around 450,000 years ago in France and England. The distinctive handax developed by the Chellean peoples sets a new standard of human skill. This culture is later called Abbevillian for it was in evidence at both French sites in Abbeville and Chelles.

Clactonian Cultures Refers to Lower Paleolithic technological areas in northwest Europe. Clactonian industries are found in the same deposits as the *coup-de-poing* (which see). They are probably contemporary with Chellean and Lower Acheulian times. Flake tools, rough scrapers, and disks are found.

Cortical surface area The gray matter over most of the mass of the brain.

Coup-de-poing A flint hand ax characteristic of the Chellean, Acheulian, and Mousterian cultures. The coup-de-poing is a superficially flaked core-tool probably used as the first formal implement, thus its importance in archeological discussions. These heavy triangular artifacts were probably for general utility use and for hunting. Coups-de-poing became extinct in Europe around the Mousterian Age. Their lower and upper faces are trimmed and there is a sharp edge between the faces. The two major types of coup-de-poing are pointed and pear shaped, and flat and oval. The flat, oval type was probably mainly used for scraping and cutting, and the pointed kind for stabbing and piercing hides before skinning. The first recorded discovery of a coup-de-poing was made in 1690, by some workmen digging at Gray's Inn, London. It was believed to be of Roman origin. About 100 years later, similar implements were found by John Frere in Suffolk. In 1825 John MacEnery began digging in Torquay, and in 1828 Townsend found implements with some Quarternary fauna in France. In 1837 Boucher de Perthes published his famous account of the discovery of chipped flints in the Somme alluvial deposits. The coup-de-poing is also called the hand ax or fist ax.

Cranial capacity The interior volume of the cranium (skull) measured in cubic centimeters.

Cranium The skull exclusive of the lower jaw and the facial bones. The cranium, also called the brain case, fits around the brain closely enough to provide a sign of the individual's cerebral development. As the cranium increases proportionately, the facial part of the skull seems to withdraw below it. As the front part of the human animal's brain developed, the forehead became vertical. Since the human brain case is globular and large in surface, the muscles of mastication and the neck muscles can be attached without any special flanges or crests such as are found in lower animals.

Cro-Magnon A variety of *Homo sapiens* dominant in Western Europe during the last half of the fourth glaciation, often referred to as the first modern man. The western European population was associated with the Aurignacian and later cultures. Remains were first found in 1868, in the rock shelter of Cro-Magnon in the village of Les Eyzies, Dordogne, France (Cro-Magnon is French for great hole). Five skeletons were found there, although similar findings have been made in Western Europe for many years. It is believed that the Cro-Magnon were absorbed into later populations. This type was fairly tall and had a larger cranial capacity than modern man, with a high forehead and prominent chin. Cro-Magnon is probably the prehistoric *Homo sapiens* of whom we know the most. Their culture went through the Aurignacian, Solutrean, and Magdalenian stages. There were many stone instruments, and flint chipping reached its highest development among them. Reindeer horn, bone, and ivory were also used to make various implements. Cro-Magnon dwellings were in rock shelters and caves, where the dead were ritually buried. Red ocher was found in many graves, although the exact significance of this is not known. Ornaments such as necklaces were in the graves of the period, and the fine arts, including painting, drawing, and sculpture, probably first appeared in the Aurignacian period.

Cultivation The intentional tilling of the soil for

either/both the planting of seed and the nurture of indigenous growth for the purpose of growing food. Three primary kinds of cultivation include dry, shifting, and wet cultivation. Shifting cultivation means cultivating a plot for a few croppings until it becomes exhausted, then moving a settlement to a new plot to start again. Dry cultivation means cultivation in which rain provides the necessary moisture. Using this technique, most plots can produce only a few croppings before becoming exhausted. Wet cultivation means crop cultivation in which springs, rivers, or torrents provide all or part of the necessary moisture. In all three instances, cultivation means the intentional effort of individuals in tilling soil for the purpose of raising food.

Cultural Ages A major subdivision in the history of cultural evolution. The term has been condemned as confusing, since it suggests that a given chronological period had a homogeneity of culture. Even groups living near each other at the same time may be from different "ages," as in England after 20,000 years ago, when warrior herdsmen from the Bronze age, Neolithic farmers, and Mesolithic hunters lived near each other. The early divisions into Paleolithic (Old Stone), Neolithic (New Stone), Heliolithic (Copper), Bronze, and Iron ages are no longer seen as regular and clear-cut divisions.

Darwinian evolutionary science Modern biological sciences based on the accepted insights of Charles Darwin. No serious scientific work can be done without this perspective.

DNA In 2004, researchers from the Max Planck Institute

for Evolutionary Anthropology in Germany completed tests for the presence of intact mitochondrial DNA (which see) in skeletal material from 24 Neanderthals and 40 early modern *Homo sapiens*. They found it in four of the Neanderthals and five of the early modern humans. These individuals lived 60,000 to 30,000 years ago in Central and Western Europe. The nucleotide (which see) sequences that were analyzed indicated that early modern humans were significantly different genetically from Neanderthals. It was estimated that only about 25 percent of the Neanderthal sequences were shared with their early modern human contemporaries. Critics have pointed out, however, that these differences between Neanderthals and modern humans could be accounted for by what is known as genetic drifting which caused rapid changes in gene pool frequencies and that *Homo sapiens* living at their time might not have been very different from Neanderthals genetically. Additional evidence came to light as a result of the 1999 discovery of a four-year-old child's skeleton in Portugal dating to about 25,000 years ago. He had a mixture of Neanderthal and modern human anatomical characteristics suggesting that he had been a hybrid. This was 3,000 to 4,000 years after the last known Neanderthal about 28,000 years ago. The implication is that some of the Neanderthals interbred with modern humans resulting in what is known as "gene flow" between the populations. If this is true, then the genetic difference between us and them must not have been as great as would be expected between two distinct species. In other words, this would suggest that the Neanderthals were a variety of *Homo sapiens* rather than a distinct species and that at least some people from Europe and possibly southwest Asia may share some Neanderthal genes. In November of

2006, a team of scientists for the first time analyzed DNA from the nuclei of cells preserved in 37,000 year old Neanderthal fossils which has now laid the foundation for determining the entire sequence of the Neanderthal genome within about two years. Dr. Edward M. Rubin of the Lawrence Berkeley Natural Laboratory at the University of California said, "We're going to be able to learn about their biology and learn about things we could never learn from the bones and the artifacts we have." The size of the total Neanderthal population appears to have diminished steadily beginning around 35,000 years ago. The last secure date for a Neanderthal site was about 28,000 years ago as we have said. What happened to them is not clear yet but it has been suggested that their relatively abrupt disappearance roughly coincides with the arrival and growth in population size of modern humans in Europe and, very possibly, they were not able to compete effectively with the technologically more advanced and numerically larger newcomer population.

Domestication The supervised control of groups of animals by human beings. The breeding of such animals is controlled, and they are protected against other animals and weather, in addition to being fed regularly and having their mobility restricted. Features which are desirable for human purposes are developed by progressive breeding under artificial conditions. Some of the characteristics which often result from domestication include excess fat on the rump, short jaw, drooping ears, and depigmentation or melanism. Domesticating animals is an artificial process which is probably linked with the growth of agriculture. Taking care of animals properly is time consuming and early food gathering communities could not spare persons for domestication, assuming that taming techniques were known. Domestication also refers to the regular growing of plants.

Ehringsdorf A cranium reported in 1928 from Ehringsdorf near Weimar, Germany. It was found near Mousterian implements and tropical flora and fauna. It probably dates from the second half of the last interglacial, about 120,000 years ago. It is slightly more like the modern human skull than the Steinheim skull, with a brain capacity of around 1,450 cc., a substantial forehead, rounded occipital area, and fairly high vault, while the lower jaw and eyebrow ridges have some primitive qualities.

Epistemology That branch of philosophy which investigates the origin, structure, methods, validity and limits of knowledge.

Ethos The values of an intentional community embodied in its worldview and expressed in its myths and rituals.

Finger tracings The earliest indications of prehistoric peoples' aesthetic sensibilities demonstrated in their formalized tracing of images in clay by use of their fingers. Many illustrations of this primitive art form exist in the caves of southern France where the art form called stratiation is most evident.

Flint burins A flake tool for sculpting or engraving. Basically it consists of a blade with the sides sliced obliquely at one end so that they form a narrow chisel edge when they meet. There were over 20 major kinds of burin. They were especially associated with the Upper Paleolithic cultures. The burin is pointed by a facet being removed along an edge in such a manner that it can be repointed again merely by removing another facet.

Flint chipping Shaping stones by chipping them. In the anvil method, the stone is struck on a fixed stone and held in the hand. In the hammer method, the stone is held by the feet or hands, or by wood or fiber strips, or buried in the ground; it splits differently according to the manner in which the stroke is cushioned. The bipolar technique consists of holding the stone on another stone, thus combining the hammer and anvil methods and giving rise to bulbs of percussion.

Flint-knapping technique A method used in the Paleolithic age of shaping a stone using a tool to chip away the flint edging to make for a sharp or cutting side.

Galileo (1564-1642) The Italian astronomer and physicist who demonstrated the truth of the Copernican theory that the planets revolve around the sun and that the turning of the earth on its axis accounts for the apparent rising and setting of the stars and sun with the telescope; condemned for heresy by the Inquisition and burned at the stake, one more graphic instance of religion taking precedence over science.

Glaciation The covering of large parts of the earth by a thick layer of snow and ice. Glaciation makes it difficult for most flora and for some fauna to grow. Early Europe has been covered by four ice ages – Günz, Mindel, Riss, and Würm – named after four Swiss streams. Glaciers still exist in parts of the north and the Alps. It is believed that *Homo sapiens* appeared in the intermediary period between the Günz and Mindel Eras. The term glacier was coined by McLennan. The poet-naturalist Schimper first wrote on a Great Ice Age, and the naturalist Agassiz confirmed his findings by studying the Swiss glaciers and their effects. The four extremes of the Glacial Age have been correlated with three or more glacial extremes in England, northern Germany, and Russia. There is some doubt about the number and contemporaneity of the successive glacial stages and their relation to climatic changes. The second and third glaciations were probably the most severe and were probably separated by an intermediate warm phase which may have exceeded all the others up until that time. The onset of the first glaciation was preceded by a long period in which the temperature gradually fell; and the final glaciation was divided into a number of small oscillations of lessening intensity. It has been suggested that the Glacial Age can be regard as a series of temperature undulations that increased to a maximum and then diminished. Some authorities have even suggested that the period called post-glacial is perhaps merely an intermission between the last glaciation and the one yet to come. The four major glaciations began, respectively, 600,000, 500,000, 250,000, and 120,000 years ago, with the last reaching its terminal period about 20,000 years ago.

Historico-temporal legitimacy A community's basis for confidence in its way of life based upon its certainty with respect to the actual historical emergence and endurance of itself re-affirmed in its worldview and ethos, rituals and myths.

Hominid Refers to the human being, from Pleistocene times onward. Also, the family of the Hominidae, which currently includes only the species *Homo sapiens*. The hominids originated in either Africa or Asia. It is possible that the Hominidae originated in the early Pliocene Period.

Hominidal sequencing The arranging of hominidal species so as to imply or suggest a logical progression from one genus of *Homo* to another. Much argument and little agreement has occurred over the past one hundred years in terms of the exact sequencing of the various branches of the *Homo spp.* though there is no argument that the species has evolved over time from less developed to more developed varieties.

Hominoid A fossil type which is human-like but not recognized as fully a human being.

Homo erectus Earliest known members of the genus *Homo* and in the direct line of descent of *Homo sapiens* from the Lower Pleistocene period and formerly called *Pithecanthropus erectus*.

Homo habilis A fossil hominid found in Bed 1 at Olduvai Gorge in East Africa by the Leakeys. It may be either an advanced form of Australopithecine or the earliest known member of the genus *Homo*. The word means "handy man" or "tool maker" and the debate continues as to its exact location on the evolutionary chain but there is no debate as to its importance in the discussion.

Homo hermeneuticus A conceptually descriptive characterization of the human animal given the strong inclination to interpret his living space and the meaning of his life in it.

Homo sapiens sapiens The species to which all extant humans belong. First found in the Upper Paleolithic, the skull is thin-walled and the face light-boned. The forehead is high and the head dome-shaped. The hair is thrown into high relief because the face is pulled in under the forehead. There are cheek hollows not found in Neanderthal man and a chin. *Homo sapiens* appeared with Aurignacian (which see) culture, in which flint blades were the most important tools. In the middle of the Upper Paleolithic, *Homo sapiens* entered the Solutrean period (which see), characterized by excellent flint working. The Magdalenian period (which see), which followed, saw the slight deterioration of stonework and the rise of bone for tools. In Europe, *Homo sapiens* with his Aurignacian culture probably drove the Musterian Neanderthals away as they overlapped by as much as 18,000 to 20,000 years. *Homo sapiens sapiens* is the sole existing species of the genus *Homo*.

Homo politicus Distinctive characterization of *Homo sapiens sapiens* and their ancestors with special reference to the strong inclination to cultivate a formalized mechanism for the exercise of corporate and community power and authority over members of an intentional grouping.

Homo Rhodesiensis A possible type of *Homo neanderthalensis* found in 1921 in Northern Rhodesia. The specimen was an almost complete skull and some leg bones. It had a large face and teeth. The specimen is also called Rhodesian Man and Broken Hill Man. It was not buried and was found in a cave shaft. The skull was thick, long and low. Rhodesian Man had a brain capacity of 1,300 to 1,500 cc. The brows and palate are very large. The mouth is human, but the cranium is low and the **brow ridges** are more passive than in any other human skull. The jaw, palate, and brain case are Neanderthaloid, while the foramen magnum and some of the nose and ear features differ somewhat from Neanderthal. The antiquity of Rhodesian Man is not clear. The artifacts are late Lavallois while the freshness of the skull and the associated animal bones seem to indicate considerable modernity, as do the caries. Rhodesian man probably became extinct because he was too specialized.

Homo socialis "Sociable Man" or "Party Animal" is the characterization of *Homo sapiens sapiens* with special reference to their "social" character as a distinguishing behavioral drive or force in their endurance.

Homo soloensis A type of fossil man, represented by eleven skulls without facial skeleton found in 1931 by W.F.F. Oppenoorth, near the Solo River in Java. These skulls are regarded as an enlarged Pithecanthropus type and they also have much in common with Sinanthropus. *Homo soloensis* is probably from an era comparable to the third European interglacial period. The brow ridges are like those of *Homo Rhodesiensis*, although not so large. The posture was also like Rhodesian man's. The foramen magnum is like that of *Homo sapiens*, and the brain volume was around 1,150 - 1,300 cc. The one shin bone found is quite modern. The Solo man probably became extinct because he was too specialized and appeared to have lived in solitary fashion except, of course, for mating.

Homo symbolicum A conceptually descriptive

characterization of the human animal as the maker and user of symbols.

Horticultural wisdom The corporate shared communal knowledge of flora which includes both nutritional and medical usage and application thought indispensable for the survival of prehistoric human communities and in modern times again greatly valued by some segments of society as having enduring value for health and well-being.

Hunting and gathering A very early and still somewhat enduring subsistence communal living style consisting of merely hunting game and gathering plants for the survival of a family, clan, or tribe. The earliest form of Paleolithic economics.

Huxley, Sir Julian Sir Julian Sorell Huxley (1887-1975) was an English biologist and writer who was educated at Oxford and taught there. He held teaching and research appointments at King's College, London, during which time he was Secretary of the Zoological Society of London as well as President of the National Union of Scientific Workers. A wider audience beyond the academy knows him as the first Director-General of the United Nations Educational, Scientific, and Cultural Organization (UNESCO). A prolific writer and popularizer of scientific knowledge, he is very well known as the grandson of Thomas Henry Huxley who was the aggressive proponent of evolution and the highly acclaimed "bulldog" for Charles Darwin. Sir Julian was knighted by Queen Elizabeth II in 1958. He is considered one of the most important spokespersons for the secular humanist movement.

Ideology The formulation of a concept or thought system which is sufficiently strong as to merit fostering, exploring, testing, and developing.

Imagination The capacity particularly developed among humans to form mental images of what is not actually present or even actually real but envisioned in the mind such that it appears as potentially real.

Interglacial Periods Those large blocks of time falling between the height of each of the four major glacial periods. These were very active periods for evolutionary development among plant and animal life and the last one was of particular relevance to the evolution of modern humans.

Kant, Emanuel (1724-1804) was born and died in Konigsberg. Studied in the Leibniz-Wolffian philosophy under Martin Knutzen. Also studied and taught astronomy, mechanics and theology. The influence of Newton's physics and Lockean psychology vied with his Leibnizian training. Kant's personal life was that of a methodic pedant, touched with Rousseauistic piety and Prussian rigidity. He scarcely traveled 40 miles from Konigsberg in his lifetime, disregarded music, had little esteem for women, and cultivated few friends apart from the Prussian officials he knew in Konigsberg. In 1775, he became tutor in the family of Count Keyserling. In 1766, he was made under-librarian, and in 1770 obtained the chair of logic and metaphysics at the University of Konigsberg. Heine has made classical the figure of Kant appearing for his daily walk with clock-like regularity. But his very wide reading compensated socially for his narrow range of travel, and made him an interesting conversationalist as well as a successful teacher.

Kierkegaard, Soren Thought to be the father of modern Christian existentialism.

Levalloisian-Mousterian A flake industry found in West Europe associated with the Middle and Upper Acheulian materials as well as with Mousterian tools dating from about 200,000 years ago. Its primary characteristic was its persistent use of flake-made tools prepared from stone cores.

Ligatures A single compound letter which combines the major features of each component in the compound letter, e.g., successive occurrences of "f" are printed as the ligature "ff."

Lower Paleolithic Age Period covering the time from about 550,000 to 70,000 years before the modern era and including the pre-Chellean, Chellean, and Acheulian stages (see elsewhere for descriptions). It is also called the Lower Old Stone Age by non-technically trained archeological amateurs. Fire was not used during this period, nor were animals or plants domesticated. The Paleolithic peoples were probably hunters. The *coup-de-poing* (which see elsewhere) became smaller and smaller and more regular flakes were produced during this period. Later, tools were produced by roughing out a core so that flakes could be struck from it and made into tools by retouching. Two culture areas, the Southwest-Asiatic-African-West Europe and the East-Europe (and perhaps North-Asiatic) were discernible.

Magdalenian culture Dates from about 15,000 years ago in western Europe and as far east as Russia which is often considered the final culture of the Upper Paleolithic Age in Europe. The last level of the Upper Paleolithic Age in its European development, it was characterized by the increase in antler and bone working, such as the bone harpoon head; and from the prevalence of reindeer it is sometimes called the Reindeer Age. It lasted from some 15,000 years ago more or less and ended about 10,000 years ago. Many think long blades date from this period. Ivory was used for carving. The art work of this period was representational. The climate was fairly arctic and was damper than in Solutrean times and steppe conditions were not so rigorous. Many large animals died off after the Ice Age ended and man lived on lake shores or grassy land. Magdalenian culture is largely a French development, although it ranged from Bavaria to parts of Spain. In Magdalenian home art, single geometric patterns were used, but animal engravings were also common. The fifth Magdalenian period had the best engravings, with degeneration appearing in the sixth period. Conventionalization occurred with increasing frequency toward the end of Magdalenian times. The graphic arts also included polychrome paintings. Composite implements, like the harpoon and atlatl (spear thrower) were common. There was more use of organic materials, shaped in a variety of ways.

Malar The zeugmatic bone which constitutes much of the outer and lower borders of the eye's bony orbit quite pronounced in pre-*Homo sapiens sapiens* such as Neanderthals and earlier varieties of *Homo erectus*.

Masticatory apparatus All that is necessary for the

chewing of food including the tongue, jaw, mouth, teeth, and throat. The chewing of food has gone through a major evolution from the early apes who even today chew up and down whereas the human animal rotates the jaw in the chewing of food. The type of food itself has participated in this evolution.

Maxillary prognathism The maxillae is the upper jaw consisting of two bilateral bones. It composes the bony support of the middle portion of the face forming part of the eye orbits, nasal fossae, most of the palate, and part of the cheekbones. Incomplete fusion of the maxillae leads to cleft palate. Prognathensis is the protrusion of the jaw, called commonly the jutting jaw, of apes and early pre-humans and still appears in various forms among modern humans.

Memory The capacity to recall past experiences, particularly developed among humans.

Mesolithic Age The Azilian, Tardenoisian, Maglemosian, Campignian and Capsian periods, from about 25,000 years ago to about 12,000 years ago. The culture is an extension of Paleolithic. Modern weather replaced the glacial, making a change in culture necessary. As a result of the new development, European Mesolithic culture looks meager; and though such inventions as pottery and the bow appeared, their full import was felt only after the Mesolithic. The sparse food supply is linked with the populations' scattering out. Shellfish, waterfowl, and hares were typical of the humbler food used. Implements grew smaller. The European Mesolithic cultures are divisible into those, like the Azilian and Tardenoisian, which had no ax and used no timber, and those middle and late Mesolithic cultures, like the Maglemosian, Campignian, and Asturtian in which the ax was used. Dogs are found with the Azilian and Tardenoisian. Pottery stems from the Campignian period of the European Mesolithic.

Microliths A very fine small pressure-flaked flint from the Neolithic, Epipaleolithic, and Magdalenian eras. Microliths were used for cutting, sewing, drawing, scraping, etc., and indicated a careful precision in the creator of the microliths.

Middle Paleolithic Age Period of cultural history from the third interglacial through the fourth glacial epoch (see elsewhere). This period probably started about 125,000 years ago and lasted to about 15,000 years ago. From a cave in Le Moustier, France, it is also called the Mousterian period (see elsewhere). This period saw the rise of Neanderthaloids (see elsewhere) and is sometimes called the period of the Cave Man by amateurs. Finer flint implements appeared at this time. Bone tools, scraper tools, and fire were also characteristic. Man had a stable residence and buried the dead, suggesting the belief in an afterlife and religion. Along with the dead, flints, red ocher, and uneaten cooked meat were often buried. Although the dead were buried inside the caves, Neanderthal peoples did not live there, but under the overhanging ledge and on the outer platforms. There may have been a curtain of animal skins used to keep out the wind and rain. The flint industry over most of habitable Europe became fairly uniform, as well as in nearby parts of Asia and Africa. This was the period of maximum Würm glaciation (see elsewhere).

Molar dentition The evolution of the human species is directly linked to the shifting in cranial configuration and diet which, in turn, is reflected in the formation and composition of the teeth and their dentition or fit. The three teeth on top and bottom and on either side of the human mouth which are behind the premolars are called molars. They are the grinding teeth used to crush and chew food. The crowns have four or five cusps. The great apes have a medial crest which is a rise in the bone on the top of the skull to which massive muscles attached to the jaws are likewise attached. The great apes need these massive muscles because of chewing required in their diet. The human animal's diet has so radically changed that the medial crest needed to hold the massive jaw muscles is no longer needed. Molar dentition reflects the way the grinding teeth fit into each other from the top and bottom.

Mousterian Culture See "Middle Paleolithic Age" above for a discussion of this period. This is the culture most associated with Neanderthal peoples during the third interglacial and fourth glacial epochs in Europe. This was a culture which produced flake tools lighter and smaller than **Levalloisian** flake tools and reflected an intentional refinement in human artifacts.

Mousterian Industry A mainly Middle Paleolithic tool culture traditionally associated with Neanderthals between 200,000 and 40,000 years ago. This is the name archeologists have given to an ancient Middle Stone Age method of making stone tools. The Mousterian is associated with our hominid relatives the Neanderthals in Europe and both *Homo sapiens* and *Homo neanderthalensis* in Africa. These stone tools were in use between about 200,000 years ago until about 40,000 years ago, after the Acheulian (which see) industry, and about the same time as the Fauresmith tradition in South Africa. Recent DNA studies at the site of Feldhofer Cave suggest that Neanderthals and Humans had a common ancestor about 550,000 years ago. The record for the Mousterian contrasts sharply with that of the modern humans who followed. While the Neanderthals made a variety of tools in stone – some of them quite complicated – the lack of innovation over time is surprising from a modern perspective. For example, not a single tool form existed 40,000 years ago that was not already present 150,000 years earlier. There was an almost mechanical redundancy to Mousterian tools that may imply more programmed behavior than that of later peoples.

Myth A story of an ahistorical event or occurrence embodied in the self-understanding of a community employed to encompass both the worldview and ethos of that community.

Neanderthal An extinct fossil variety of early humans dominant in Europe from the second interglacial epoch to the climax of the fourth glacial, known most correctly as *Homo sapiens neandertalensis*. This human form of man has many variations, often divided into four subgroups, the Rhodesian (*Homo Rhodesiensis*), the Mousterian, or Spy, the Ehringsdorf, and the subgroup closest to modern man, including the Skhul Mount Carmel and the Galilee remains. *Homo neanderthalensis* (more common variant spelling) was first found in Gibraltar in 1848 and was intensively studied in 1936. It was named in 1864 by William King. Elements of over 100 Neanderthal remains have been found. It flourished during the third and fourth glacial periods, as mentioned above. **Classic Neanderthals** are probably from the fourth glacial advance. Their dead were buried, along with their tools. The presence of speech may be inferred owing to anatomical analysis. Mousterian culture predominated among them. Primarily because they buried their dead and because they lived fairly recently, about 150,000 to 28,000 years ago, the overlap the earliest *Homo sapiens sapiens* by as much as 12,000 years. A good deal is known about the Neanderthals and renewed interest has surfaced owing to recent developments in DNA testing.

Neanderthals, Classic (cold-adapted) Researchers have suggested that the development of Pithecanthropus' brain led to a generalized Neanderthal with two kinds of development around Acheulian times. One type had a large brain and large brow ridges, jaws, and palate, with specialized skull and teeth, and limb changes, which gave rise to the extreme Neanderthal, or classic "cold-adapted" type.

Neanderthals, Progressive (Modern) The other development saw the brain being enlarged while the brow ridges and jaws receded, the teeth became smaller, and a vertical forehead, and rounded cranium, appeared, as well as the limb characteristics of earlier Pithecanthropus. It has been suggested by recent researchers that the this line of development led from the Acheulians to modern day *Homo sapiens*.

Neolithic Age Period from 12,000 years ago, sometimes called the Late Stone Age or New Stone Age. Weaving, pottery, fine flint-working, the bow and arrow, and many metal tools were characteristic as were the wheel, a primitive pastoralism and agriculture, and a lack of iron and bronze metallurgy. The name was early applied to ground or polished implements which were found along with the bones of fairly recent animal species. The Neolithic Age ended when copper and bronze were used regularly. Others have argued that a better criterion of Neolithic would be an economy which is self-sufficient in food production. There was a change in this age from chipped to polished stone tools. The rice, maize, barley, wheat, and other cereals then domesticated are still present today. The Neolithic Age is so called because archeologists saw the grinding and polishing of stone implements instead of chipping as the hallmark. In the Near East, people gradually changed to a producer of food from a gatherer of food. While the European climate improved, North Africa and southern Asia developed a desert and dry climate so that people did not have so much space to live in and were drawn close together, especially in oases and river valleys. These groups gradually learned to live in a more settled manner and raise their own food. Neolithic culture came to Europe overland from the southeast by the Danube and its offshoots; from the North African coastal plains via the Straits of Gibraltar, to Spain, France, and England; and overland from South Russia, Poland, central Europe, and Germany. The Neolithic people colonized Greece first, probably coming from southern Anatolia. The first major building of this era was found in Jericho. It was probably a temple. Religious cultism, especially phallic and fertility cults, may have been widespread. Megalithic burial structures were constructed in the Near East and Europe, although there was probably a cultural lag in the European Neolithic.

Newton, Sir Isaac (1642-1727), English mathematician and philosopher; formulated the binomial theorem, the laws of gravity and motion, and the elements of differential calculus.

New World Monkeys The New World Monkeys live in forest and swamp areas of South and Central America. They are characterized by their flaring, widely separated nostrils, giving them the name "platyrrhine" monkeys. Many are entirely arboreal, and some have long, prehensile tails by which they hang from trees. Although other New world Monkeys spend much of their time in the trees, they do not often swing from limb to limb by their arms and have not developed the extremely long forelimbs characteristic of many Old World Monkeys.

Occipital aspects Refers to the occiput or the occipital bone which is a single bone found on the posterior-superior-inferior part of the skull. Part of the bone can usually be felt on the back of the head as the occipital prominence.

Ocher An oxide of iron mixed with earth and clay, varying in color from yellow to chocolate. The ochers occur naturally and were often used in Upper Paleolithic times in art. Red ocher appears in ceremonial burials. These colors are permanent and are still used.

Old World Monkeys They live in the arboreal and terrestrial environments of Africa and Asia but not in the western hemisphere. They are characterized by their closely spaced, downward-pointing nostrils, the presence of two, rather than three, premolars on each side of each jaw, and their lack of prehensile tails. Some are equally at home on the ground and in the trees, such as the macaques, of which there are some 50 species ranging from Gibraltar (the Barbary Ape) to Japan.

Olfactory sense The capacity to differentiate between the smells of things, pronounced in primates and particularly mammals, and only somewhat developed among humans. This sense gradually diminished within the human animal as other senses placed demands upon the size and capability of the brain.

Oligarchic imperative The socio-political principle which says that when two or three persons are together, one will eventually dominate.

Opposable digitation The ability to oppose the thumb to the fingers and to bring the finger tips into contact with the ball of the thumb. It is a characteristic distinguishing *Homo sapiens* from all other primates.

Paleodemography Attempts have been made to determine the longevity of early peoples and the French scholar, Henri Vallois, has examined two Zinjanthropus and Neanderthal remains and has suggested that the average lifespan to be about 21 years old. This low longevity rate could account for a slow rate of population increase he argues. He projected that the Upper Paleolithic population in France was at about 60,000 and in Europe as a whole at below 500,000. However, the Russian anthropologist at Harvard University, Valery Alexeev, argues with these figures, suggesting that there were never more than about 50,000 people for the whole territory of Europe. The Upper Paleolithic extends in his estimations from 40,000 to 12,000 years ago with a longevity rate of about 21 years whereas the Mesolithic period saw longevity reach to nearly 28 years.

Paleographics J. A. Cheyne has developed this term to convey "Stone Age Art." Prior to about 30,000 years ago, he says we see the beginnings of graphic activity by which he means "any activity that results in the production of visual signs in any medium." This will, he explains, incorporate what is generally referred to as art, such as pictures or figurines, as well as the production of non-figurative marks that are typically designated as signs and symbols. In Europe, this activity began in the Aurignacian (which see) and peaked in the Magdalenian (which see). These are exclusively associated with *Homo sapiens* with the possible exception of a few very ambiguous cases.

Paleolithic Age The Old Stone Age characterized by chipped stone tools. Period lasting from about 500,000 to 10,000 years during which artifacts now found along with the bones of extinct wild animals were produced by chipping. The Paleolithic Age, a name coined by Sir John Lubbock in 1865 is also called the Middle Old Stone Age, the Old Stone Age, or the Stone Age. It is often divided into various stages, ranging from the pre-Chellean to the Magdalenian and the Azilian, which were the transition to the Neolithic Age. In the Paleolithic Age, humans slowly began differentiating themselves from the animal world. They lived in small groups, perhaps often in caves, where most remains are found. Europe and Asia were in the Ice Age. Early human artifacts are usually said to have appeared during this period, along with religion.

Paleolithic Age, Upper Period lasting from about 70,000 to 20,000 years ago. It includes the Aurignacian, Solutrean, and Magdalenian (see elsewhere) stages. Bone, ivory, and flint implements were used in this era. The Cro-Magnons of this time probably had clothes made from animal skins and produced what is probably the first art. The bulk of the European Paleolithic culture was largely carried by these Cro-Magnons. Cultural diversity was probably grater than racial diversity. Long, fine knifelike flakes were also struck from a core. The bow and arrow and the domestication of the dog appeared. The Paleolithic period ended with the retreat of the last glacier.

Percussion technique Direct striking of core with a hammer-stone, giving thick bulbous flakes, or with a cylindrical (bone or wooden) hammer, giving flatter flakes. Indirect percussion or Punch technique necessitated the use of a bone or wooden punch between the hammer and the core, controlling the precision of flaking.

Pithecanthropus A hominid discovered in 1891-92 by Eugene Dubois in Java. It was regarded by Dubois as a "missing link" between apes and men with a primitive cranium but able to walk upright. A mandible, six femora, three skull parts, and other fragments have been found. It is now more commonly known as *Homo erectus* (which see).

Pleistocene The last million years of geological history, known as the age of glaciers, from which the earliest skeletal remains of man date. Except for the skull, humans were probably well developed early in this period. They probably were then about as large as they are now. A forest thinning which left gaps between groves might have led some of the prehuman arboreal apes to get used to the ground, even if only to move from one grove to another. Different foods might have made ground life interesting, until the trees came to be used less and less. It has been estimated that the Pleistocene lasted from 1,000,000 years ago to 500,000 years ago.

Polychrome Referring to being of more than one color as in pottery or cave paintings rather than monochrome which means one color only. The gradual sophistication of Upper Paleolithic artists, engaged in both *art mobilier* and *art parietal*, is reflected in their increasing use of a variety of color schemes, some quite remarkably outstanding.

Polytypic species A group of species potentially or actually interbreeding in isolation from similar groups; a species with many variations in different environments.

Portable art (art mobilier) The decorated and carved objects found in the dwelling sites of the Upper Paleolithic Age. This work was done with ivory, bone, and stone. A group of small and round statuettes, largely of women, was found from west Europe to east central Siberia. Many weapons and decorated tools date from this period. Valley deposits and floor accumulations have yielded a number of *art mobilier* finds. The term portable art is sometimes used.

Postorbital constriction The tightening constriction to the eye socket which emerged in the human skull. Neanderthals did not have such a constriction.

Power grip In the power grip, an object is held between the fingers and the palm, with the thumb reinforcing the fingers. In this position, much force can be applied. All primates are capable of the power grip and it is reported that an Orangutan has sufficient strength in its power grip to burst a coconut by squeezing it in one hand.

Precision grip The precision grip is used when an object is held between one or more fingers with the thumb fully opposed to the fingertips. Very delicate movements can be executed in this position. The human animal, using oppositional thumb/finger dexterity, has developed the precision grip to a degree not found in any other primates.

Prognathism The extent to which the jaw protrudes. *Homo sapiens* is the least prognathic mammal. Prognathism is measured by using the Frankfurt line to measure the angle between the nasion and the alveolar point or, in layman's terms, from the back of the jaw to the point of the chin.

Propitiate To cause to become favorably inclined or to win or regain the good will of another, to appease or conciliate. Often, the sacrificing of an animal or human was thought to appease the anger of the god or gods as in the case of the crucifiction of Jesus which was thought to appease and conciliate the anger of God for the world having gone wrong.

Prosimians A lemur or tarsier, often seen as a kind of halfway stage between monkeys and mammals that are not primates.

Psychodynamic expressiveness The driving motivation within an individual to act out behaviorally one's emotional feelings, often in either musical or artistic fashion.

Psychogenesis Suggesting the evolutionary processes of psychological development.

Quadrupedal locomotion Refers to the ability to walk or spring from all fours.

Ramapithecus A fossil primate of the Miocene epoch probably ancestral to later **hominid**s from India.

Reflective self-awareness That level of self-consciousness such that the individual is fully aware of himself and has the capacity to think about that awareness and act upon it.

Reflexive cognition That level of self-awareness in which the individual is aware of his capacity to think about thinking. Being aware of oneself is reflective, being aware that one is thinking about that experience is reflexive.

Ritual A re-enactment of a mythic event or saga embodying the worldview and ethos of a self-aware community.

Sartre, Jean-Paul The father of modern non-theistic existentialism.

Savanna In low latitudes, a wide zone with both

grasslands and forests. The tree growth is usually scattered.

Scrimshaw A pre-historic art form found among late Neanderthal, and early Cro-Magnons which consisted of carving on bone and ivory artistic designs ostensibly purely for aesthetic effect.

Slash and burn A Neolithic and somewhat still existing style of food getting consisting of cutting away unwanted flora in search of edible flora and the systematic use of fire to burn away unwanted growth to expose the sought after food stuffs.

Smell-brain center That portion of the brain wherein the **olfactory senses** are stored. These centers decreased during the evolutionary process within the human brain.

Sociogenesis Suggesting the evolutionary processes of social development.

Solipsism The epistemological doctrine which considers the individual self and its state the only possible or legitimate starting point for philosophical construction. It is a sub variety of idealism which maintains that the individual self of the solipsistic philosopher is the whole of reality and that the external world and other persons are representations of that self having no independent existence. In other worlds, a navel-gazing individual's self-absorption in himself at the expense of recognizing the existence of others.

Solutrean Culture The Old World Upper Paleolithic

period that succeeded the Aurignacian (which see) culture about 70,000 years ago around the time of the second maximum of the last glaciation. The name derives from the site uncovered at Le Solutre in France. It was fairly brief and was marked by a growth in making flint implements by pressure flaking and possibly by the needle. Stylized symbolic representations are found in its art. The bone industry did not continue to develop. Shouldered points and laurel and willow leaf points were widespread. The flint implements made were small and sliver like, with an all-over ripple retouch. Horse hunting was found. The Solutrean peoples remained in the plains. They probably did not go beyond the Pyrenees, except at the eastern end.

Spencer, Herbert (1820-1903) was the great English philosopher who devoted a lifetime to the formulation and execution of a plan to follow the idea of development as a first principle through all of the avenues of human thought. A precursor of Darwin with his famous notion of all organic evolution as a change "from homogeneity to heterogeneity," from the simple to the complex, he nevertheless was greatly influenced by the Darwinian hypothesis and employed its arguments in his monumental works in biology, psychology, sociology and ethics. He aimed to interpret life, mind and society in terms of matter, motion and force. In politics, he evidenced from his earliest writings a strong bias for individualism.

Stereoscopic vision The capacity to see three dimensional objects owing to the situating of the eyes in front of the face rather than to either side. Fish see two dimensional objects whereas monkeys and humans see three dimensions thereby allowing for a more correct assessment of the environment in terms of movement and location. This was crucial in the survival of the human animal.

Stratiation The use of the fingers or other multiple aligned instruments for the making of artistic designs using parallel lines common among early human aesthetic expression on both cave walls and bone.

Supraorbital tori The supraorbital torus is a bone ridge above the orbits of the eye sockets sometimes simply called the "brow ridge" (which see).

Taurodontism Large pulp cavities in the molar teeth so that the pulp cavities are deep and extended to the roots which fuse into a kind of stump instead of being long and separate. It is characteristic of Neanderthals and is still in residual form found among the Inuit peoples of Alaska and Canada.

Theologians The practitioners of theology, which is the systematization of a faith-community's understanding of the will and nature of their supreme being and their responsibility to that being in the living of their lives. Theologians articulate the formalized understanding of that relationship.

Taxonomy Scientific classification, particularly as applied in biology to organisms.

Transcendental legitimacy That to which a community appeals for self-validation and authentification which lies outside the phenomenal realm of experience but constitutes a force intruding in and accessible to the appeals of an intentional community.

Unknowable In the philosophy of Herbert Spencer (which see), that which is not now nor ever shall be grasped and understood through human inquiry. Scientific inquiry cannot enter into a discovery of any component of the Unknowable for by definition that which is unknowable is unknowable. To this category Spencer attributed religious belief. He was not an atheist but an agnostic, believing that religion cannot be proved either real or unreal. Religion is the domain of the Unknowable so there is nothing to discuss or explore.

Unknown In the philosophy of Herbert Spencer (which see), that which is not now but will with effort eventually come to be grasped and understood through human inquiry. Scientific inquiry is constantly reducing the mass of the Unknown while at the same time increasing that mass with new discoveries. The Unknown is that which is not yet known, not that which is completely unknowable.

Verbal acuity A refined capacity to express nuances of communication through sound generated by vocal effort as in human conversation.

Visual cortex That portion of the brain wherein the visual capabilities of the brain are located. This area continued to increase in value to the pre-human ancestry in direct proportion to the decline of the olfactory senses.

Wilson, Edward O. was born June 10, 1929, in Birmingham, Alabama, and is an entomologist and biologist known for his work on evolution and sociobiology and, by some, is called the "father of biodiversity." After earning both a B.A. and M.A. from the University of Alabama, he received his Ph.D. from Harvard University and is a specialist in ants, in particular their use of pheromones for communication. Today, Wilson is the Pellegrino University Research Professor Emeritus at Harvard University. Hailed as "the new Darwin" and one of "America's 25 Most Influential People" by *Time Magazine*, he has twice received the Pulitzer Prize.

Worldview The external world as perceived by an intentional community which embodies its sense of origin and destiny with particular reference to transcendental legitimacy.

Würm glaciation The fourth, and last, glacial period in Europe, probably extending from about 75,000 to 25,000 years ago (see **Glaciation** above).

Appendices

A. Trends in the Evolution of the Primate as Seen in the Skull
B. Cranial Capacity from Chimpanzee to *Homo erectus*
C. Venus of Willendorf
D. Taxonomic Inventory of the Hominids
E. The Pleistocene Time Scale
F. Upper Paleolithic tools
G. Skulls from Australopithecus to *Homo sapiens*
H. Major Cold and Warm Periods of the Pleistocene
I. Feet and Hand Skeletons from Lemurs to *Homo sapiens*
J. Cave Painting of the Upper Paleolithic from Northern Spain
K. Physical Characteristics of *Homo erectus*
L. Time Scale for the Evolution of the Primates
M. Primate Grips
N. Vocal Apparatus of the Neanderthal and Modern Human
O. Lower Limbs of the Gorilla and *Homo sapiens*

Appendix A
Trends in the Evolution of the Primate as Seen in the Skull

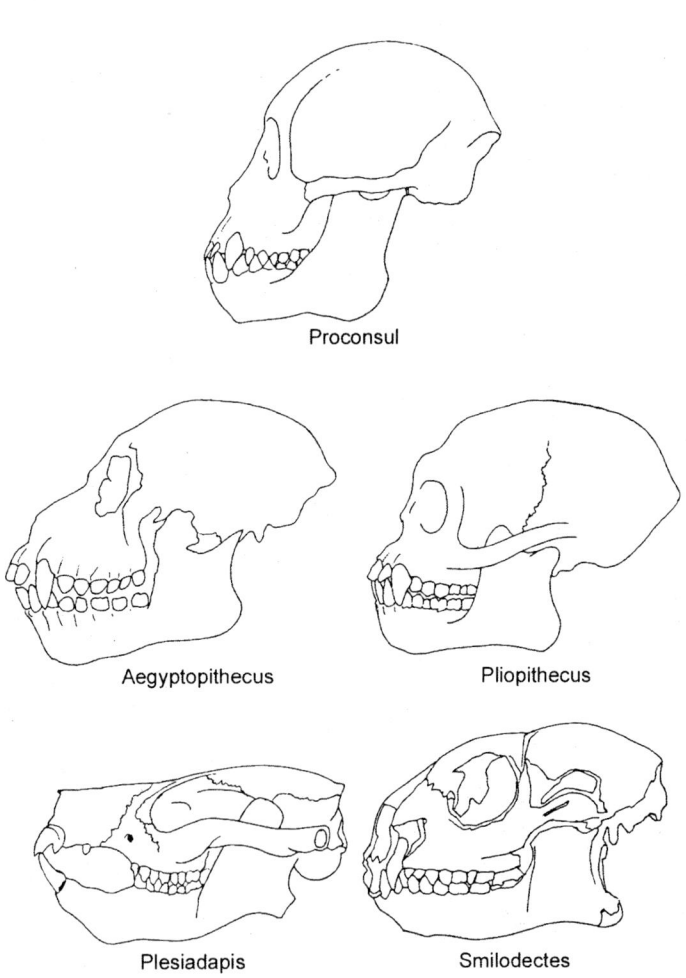

Appendix B
Cranial Capacity from Chimpanzee to *Homo erectus*

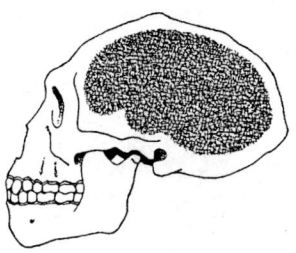

HOMO ERECTUS
973.7 cc.

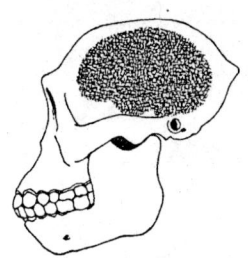

AUSTRALOPITHECUS
507.9 cc.

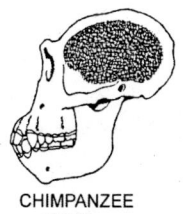

CHIMPANZEE
393.8 cc.

Appendix C
Venus of Willendorf

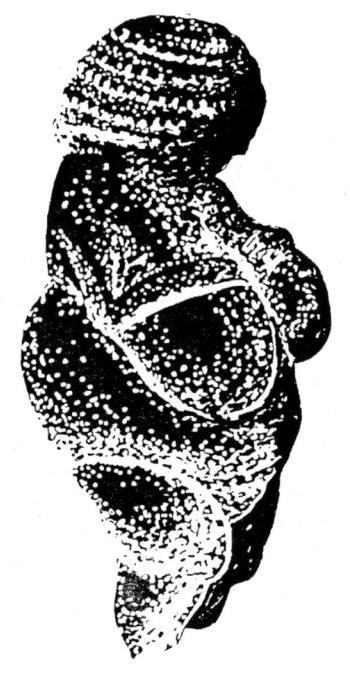

Appendix D
Taxonomic Inventory of the Hominids

Genus	Species	Subspecies
Homo	*sapiens*	*sapiens* *neandertalensis* *steinheimensis*
	erectus	*rhodesianensis* *soloensis* *pekinensis* *mauritanicus* *erectus*
	habilis(?)	
Australopithecus	*robustus* *africanus*	

Source: B. Campbell, "Quantitative Taxonomy and Human Evolution," in S.L. Washburn (ed.), *Classification and Human Evolution*, pp. 66-69.

Appendix E
The Pleistocene Time Scale

Time (years before present)	Pleistocene Division	Stage
Present – 100,000	Upper Pleistocene	IV Glacial (Würm)
100,000 – 200,000	Upper Pleistocene	3. Interglacial
200,000 – ~350,000	Middle Pleistocene	III Glacial (Riss)
~350,000 – ~620,000	Middle Pleistocene	2. Interglacial
~620,000 – ~750,000	Middle Pleistocene	II Glacial (Mindel)
~750,000 – ~930,000	Lower Pleistocene	1. Interglacial
~930,000 – 2,000,000	Lower Pleistocene	I Glacial (Günz) / Villafranchian

Appendices 151

Appendix F
Upper Paleolithic Tools

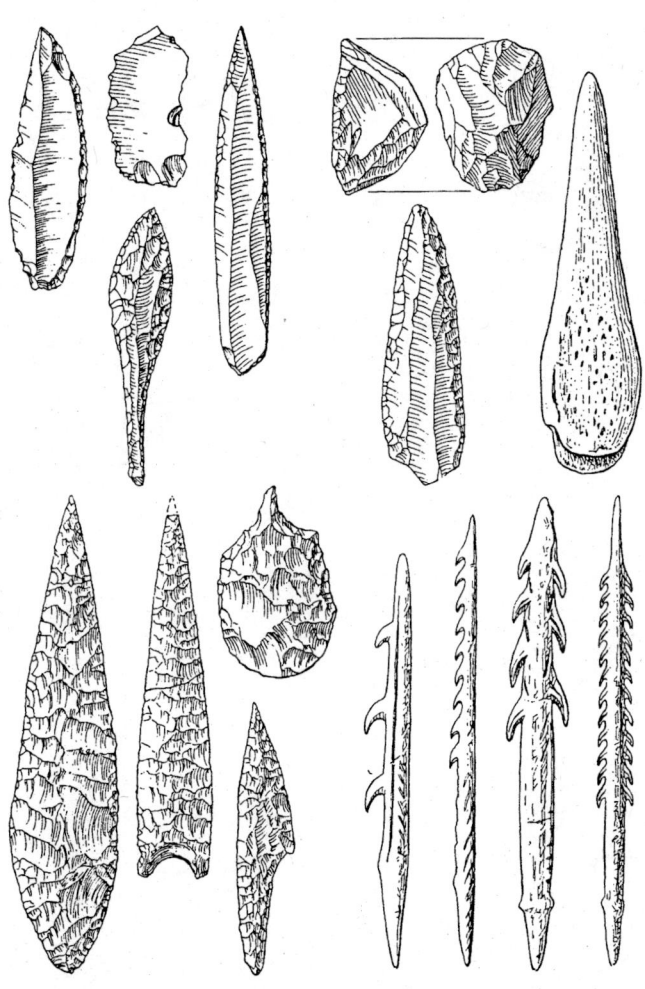

Appendix G
Skulls from Australopithecus to *Homo sapiens*

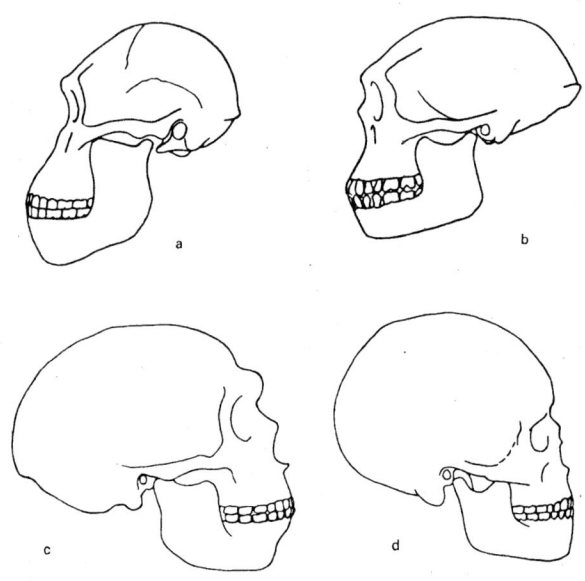

Skulls of:
a. *Australopithecus*
b. *Homo erectus* (*Pithecanthropus*)
c. *Homo neanderthalensis*
d. *Homo sapiens*

Appendix H
Major Cold and Warm Periods of the Pleistocene

Period	Glaciations and Interglacials	Major Subdivisions
Upper Pleistocene	Würm Glaciation	Würm III (Late Würm): Cold, with two short insterstadials (Bølling and Allerød) Würm II (Middle Würm or 'pleniglacial'): Very cold, with two interstadials (perhaps merging into one in some areas) Würm I (Early Würm): Cold, with two minor interstadials
Upper Pleistocene	Last Interglacial (often called Eemian)	(probably included one or more colder spells)
Middle Pleistocene	Riss Glaciation	Riss II: Interstadial (sometimes called Inter-Riss) Riss I
Middle Pleistocene	'Great' Interglacial (often called Hoxnian)	(certainly included at least one colder spell)
Lower Pleistocene	Mindel Glaciation	Mindel II: Interstadial (sometimes called Inter-Mindel) Mindel I
Lower Pleistocene	First Interglacial	
Lower Pleistocene	Günz Glaciation	Günz II: Interstadial Günz I
Basal Pleistocene	(Various Pre- Günz cold phases can be detected in parts of the northern hemisphere, but are not yet known or understood in detail.)	
Pliocene Period		

Appendix I
Feet and Hand Skeletons of (a) lemur, (b) macaque, (c) gorilla, (d) *Homo sapiens*, and (e) foot of Australopithecus

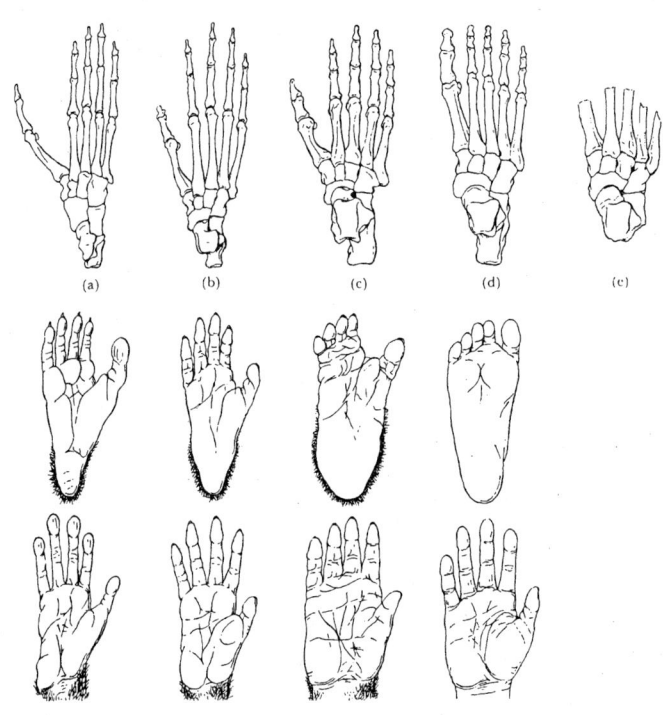

(Adapted in part from Adolph H. Shultz, *The Life of Primates*, New York: Universe Books, 1969 and W. E. LeGros Clark, 1959.)

Appendices 155

Appendix J
Cave painting of the Upper Paleolithic from Northern Spain

A more sophisticated cave painting of the Upper Paleolithic from the roof of the Altamira cave in Northern Spain showing a bison above and galloping bear below. (The Bettmann Archive)

Appendix K
Physical Characteristics of *Homo erectus*

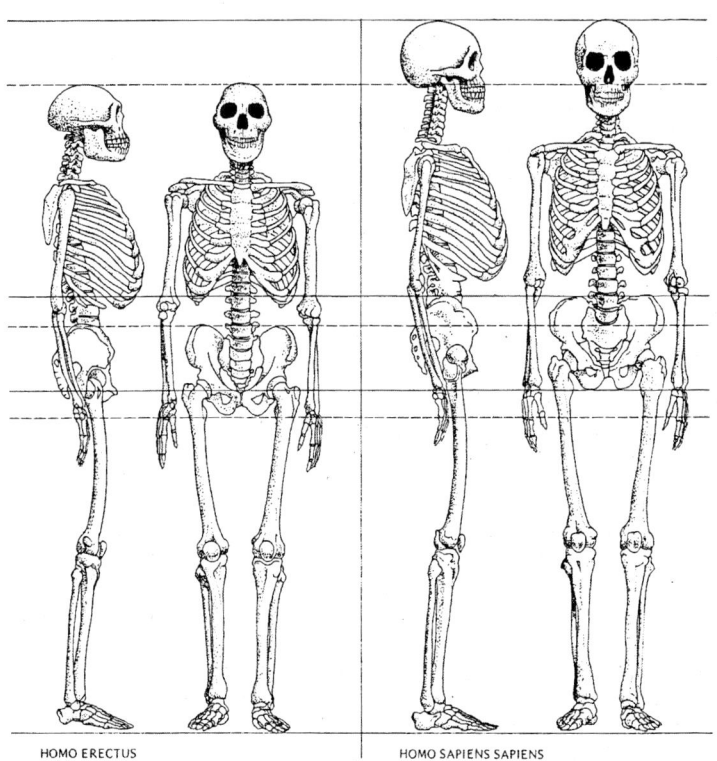

HOMO ERECTUS   HOMO SAPIENS SAPIENS

Appendix L
Time Scale for the Evolution of the Primates

Epoch	Approximate years B.P. (Before Present)	Types of primates
Pleistocene	10,000 – 2,500,000	*Homo sapiens* *Homo erectus* *Australopithecus*
Pliocene	2,500,000 – 13,000,000	*Australopithecus* *Ramapithecus* *Oreopithecus*
Miocene	13,000,000 – 25,000,000	*Kenyapithecus* *Prononsul* *Pliopithecus* *Dryopithecus*
Oligocene	25,000,000 – 36,000,000	*Propliopithecus* *Parapithecus* *Oligopithecus*
Eocene	36,000,000 – 58,000,000	Tarsiers Lemurs
Paleocene	58,000,000 – 63,000,000	Prosimians like tree shrews or lemurs

158 "In The Beginning..."

Appendix M
Primate Grips

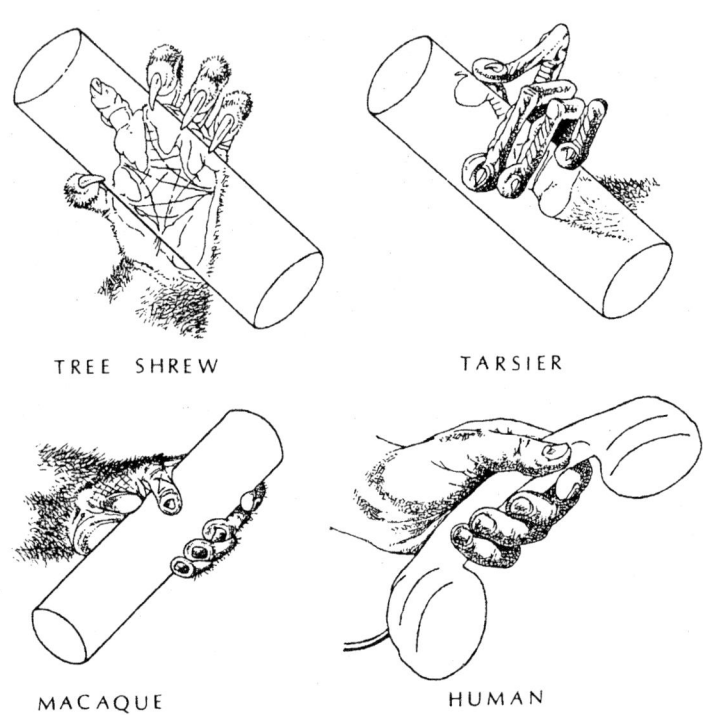

TREE SHREW

TARSIER

MACAQUE

HUMAN

Appendix N
Vocal Apparatus of the Neanderthal and Modern Human

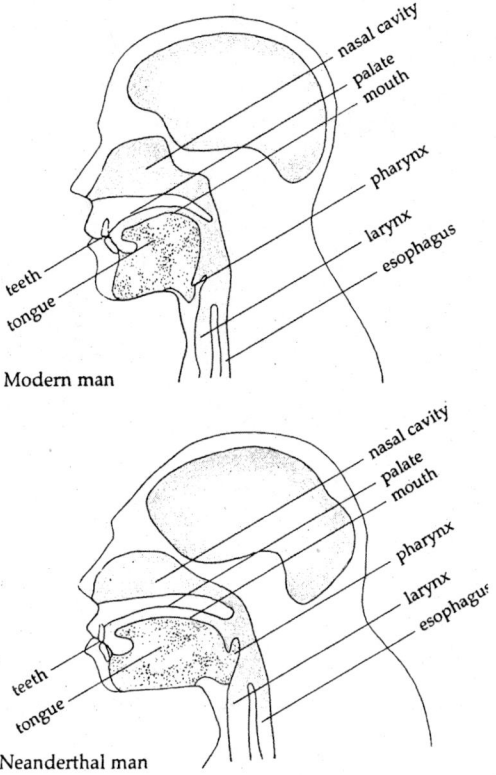

The vocal apparatus of a modern human and Neanderthal man compared. The latter had a larger and less mobile tongue than modern human and his larynx was positioned higher in the throat. Thus he was unable to make the same range of sounds, and so talk and communicate as effectively as modern human.

Appendix O
Lower Limbs of the Gorilla and *Homo sapiens*

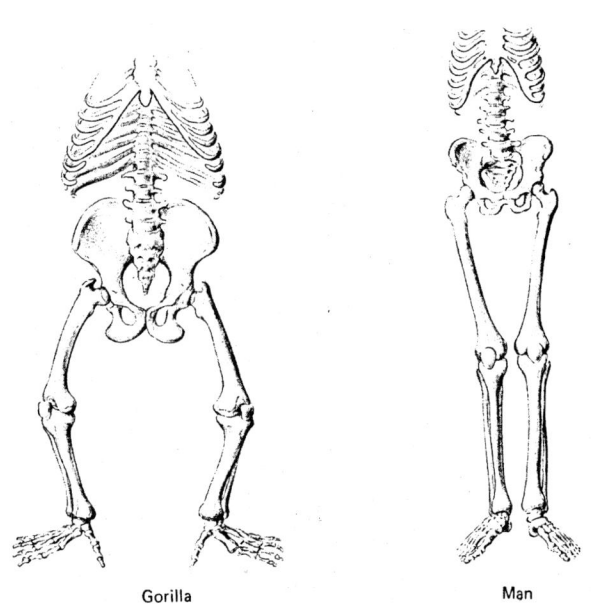

Gorilla	Man

This figure shows adaptations in the human skeleton for bipedal walking. The pelvis is both shorter and more bowl-like, allowing muscles at the front, side, and rear greater efficiency in moving the leg on the pelvis and stabilizing the pelvis on the leg.

The posture of the legs has changed in man to bring the knees and feet closer together. In the foot, the opposed or abducted, great toe is not used to support the inner side of the foot, which has stable transverse arch in man, becoming instead a powerful propulsive member.

Bibliography

Aiello, L., and C. Dean. *An Introduction to Human Evolutionary Anatomy* (London: Academic Press, 1990).

ApSimon, A. M. 1980. "The last Neanderthal in France?" in *Nature* (287: 271).

Arensburg, B. et al. 1990. "A Reappraisal of the Anatomical Basis for Speech in Middle Paleolithic Hominids," *American Journal of Physical Anthropology* (83: 137-146).

Banton, Michael, Ed. *Anthropological Approaches to the Study of Religion* (London: Tavistock Publications, 1966).

Barnouw, Victor. *An Introduction to Anthropology* (Homewood, IL: The Dorsey Press, 1972).

Berger, Peter L. and Thomas Luckmann. *The Social Construction of Reality: A Treatise in the Sociology of Knowledge* (NY: Doubleday Anchor Book, 1966).

Binford, L. *Bones: Ancient Men and Modern Myths* (NY: Academic Press, 1981).

Brace, C. Loring and Ashley Montagu, *Human Evolution: An Introduction to Biological Anthropology* (NY: Macmillan, 1977).

Braidwood, Robert J. *Prehistoric Men* (Glenview, IL: Scott, Foresman & Co., 1967).

Brothwell, D. and P. Brothwell. *Food in Antiquity: A Survey of the Diet of Early Peoples* (London: Thames and Hudson, 1969).

Campbell, Bernard G. *Human Evolution* (Chicago, IL: Aldine Publishing Co., 1974).

Campbell, B. G. *Human Ecology: The Story of Our Place in nature from Prehistory to the Present* (Chicago: Aldine Publishing, 1983).

Cronk, Lee, Napoleon Chagnon, & William Irons, Eds. *Adaptation and Human Behavior: An Anthropological Perspective* (NY: Aldine de Gruyter, 2000).

Darwin, Charles. *The Origins of Species* (NY: NY, A Mentor Book, 1958).

Dickson, D. Bruce. *The Dawn of Belief* (Tuscon, AZ: The University of Arizona Press, 1990).

Dobzhansky, Theodosius. *Genetics and the Origin of Species* (NY: Columbia University Press, 1982).

Freedman, D. G. *Human Sociobiology: A Holistic Approach* (NY: The Free Press, 1979).

Winick, Charles. *Dictionary of Anthropology* (Totowa, NJ: Littlefield, Adams & Co., 1956).

Haviland, William A. *Anthropology* (NY: Holt, Rinehart and Winston, Inc., 1974).

Haviland, William A. *Human Evolution and Prehistory* (NY: Holt, Rinehart & Winston, 1979).

Haywood, John. *The Illustrated History of Early Man* (London: Saturn books, 1995).

Hoebel, E. Adamson. *Anthropology: The Study of Man* (NY: MacGraw-Hill Books, 1972).

Howells, William. *Evolution of the Genus* Homo (Reading, MA: Addison-Wesley Publ., 1973).

Hublin, J.-J. et al. 1995. "The Mousterian Site of Zafarraya (Andalucia, Spain): Dating and Implications on the Paleolithic Peopling Process of Western Europe," in *Comptes Renduz des Seances de l'Academie des Sciences* (321: 931-7).

Hublin, J-J, et al. 1996. "A Late Neanderthal Associated with Upper Paleolithic Artefacts," *Nature* (381: 224-226).

Hunter, David E. & Phillip Whitten. *Encyclopedia of Anthropology* (NY: Harper & Row, 1976).

McKern, Sharon S. & Thomas W. McKern. *Living Prehistory: An Introduction to Physical Anthropology and Archaeology.* (Menlo Park, CA: Cummings Publishing Co., 1974).

Jaynes, J. *The Origin of Consciousness in the Breakdown of the Bicameral Brain* (Boston: Houghton Mifflin, 1978).

Larsen, C. s., R. M. Matter, and D. LO. Gebo. *Human Origins: The Fossil Record* (Prospect Heights: Waveland Press, Inc., 1991).

Leakey, Richard E. and Roger Lewin. *Origins* (NY: E. P. Dutton, 1977).

Lieberman, P. and E. S. Crelin, 1971. "On the Speech of Neanderthal Man," *Linguistic Inquiry* (2: 203-222).

Mannheim, Karl. *Ideology and Utopia: An Introduction to the Sociology of Knowledge* (NY: Harcourt, Brace and World, 1936).

Mardis, S. E. 1995. "The last Neanderthals," in *Archaeology* (48, #6: 12-13).

Mercier, N. et. Al. 1991. "Thermoluminescence Dating of the Late Neanderthal Remains from Saint-Cesaire," in *Nature* (351: 737-739).

Middleton, J. Ed. *From Child to Adult: Studies in the Anthropology of Education* (Garden City: NY:Natural History Press, 1970).

Morgan, John H. *Being Human: Perspectives on Meaning and Interpretation (Essays in Religion, Culture and Personality)* (South Bend, IN: Cloverdale Books, 2006, 2nd Edition).

Morgan, John H. *From Freud to Frankl: Our Modern Search for Personal Meaning* (Lima, OH: Wyndham Hall Press, 1987).

Morgan, John H. *In the Absence of God: Religious Humanism as Spiritual Journey (with special reference to Julian Huxley)* (South Bend, IN: Cloverdale Books, 2006).

Morgan, John H. *Naturally Good: A Behavioral History of Moral Development (from Charles Darwin to E. O. Wilson)* (South Bend, IN: Cloverdale Books, 2005).

Pfeiffer, John E. *The Emergence of Man* (NY: Harper & Row, Publs., 1969).

Pope, Georffrey G. *The Biological Bases of Human Behavior* (Boston: Allyn & Bacon, 2000).

Roe, Derek. *Prehistory: An Introduction* (Berkeley, CA: University of California Press, 1970).

Spuhler, J. N. (Ed.). *The Evolution of Man's Capacity for Culture* (Detroit, MI: Wayne State University Press, 1959).

Stein, Philip L. & Bruce M. Rowe. *Physical Anthropology* (NY: McGraw-Hill Books, 1974).

Stringer, C. B. and P. Andrews, 1988. "Genetic and Fossil Evidence for the Origin of Modern Humans," *Science* (239: 1263-68).

Stringer, C. B. and C. Gamble. *In Search of the Neanderthals: Solving the Puzzle of Human Origins* (New York: Thames and Hudson, 1993).

Ucko, Peter J. & Andree Rosenfield. *Palaeolithic Cave Art* (NY: World University Library, 1967).

Waddington, C. H. *The Ethical Animal* (Chicago, IL: University of Chicago Press, 1960).
Wallace, Anthony F. C. *Religion: An Anthropological View* (NY: Random House, 1966).
Washburn, S. L. & Ruth Moore. *Ape Into Man: A Study of Human Evolution* (Boston: Little, Brown and Co., 1974.
Wilson, Edward O. *Sociobiology: The New Synthesis* (Cambridge, MA: Harvard University Press, 1975; 2000).
Wolpoff, M. *Paleoanthropology* 2nd Edition. (Boston: McGraww-Hill, 1999).

About the Author

John H. Morgan, Ph.D.(Hartford Seminary Foundation), D.Sc.(London College of Applied Science), Psy.D. (Foundation House/Oxford), is President and the Karl Mannheim Professor of the History and Philosophy of the Social Sciences at the Graduate Theological Foundation in Indiana and the Sir Julian Huxley Professor of the History and Philosophy of Education at Cloverdale College. He has held postdoctoral appointments at Harvard, Yale, and Princeton and teaches a doctoral-level summer seminar at the University of Oxford. In 1973, he was elected to membership in both the American Anthropological Association and the American Philosophical Association. The author of over thirty books, his latest book is entitled, *In the Absence of God: Religious Humanism as Spiritual Journey (with special reference to Sir Julian Huxley).*

Index

Acheulian Culture, 2, 36, 72, 105, 111, 125, 131
agnosticism, 47, 105
Alexeev, Valery Pavlovich, 106, 134
anthropomorphism, 106
arboreal environment, 105
art mobilier. See portable art
artifact, 106
Aurignacian Culture, 4, 37, 38, 76, 77, 78, 79, 106, 107, 113, 121, 135, 136, 141
Australopithecus africanus, 5, 34, 107
Azilian, 2, 108, 127, 135

behavior, 41, 108, 162, 164
biogenesis, 22, 108
biomorphic art, 108
blade tools, 109
brow ridge, 109
bulbs of percussion, 109
burial position, 109, 110

caldarium, 110
cave painting, 4, 76, 110, 145, 155
Chatelperronian Period, 111
Chellean Culture, 2, 105, 111, 112, 125, 135

Chellean handax, 105, 111
Clactonian Cultures, 58, 111
cortical surface area, 111
coup-de-poing, 112
cranium, 112
Cranial capacity, 112
Cro-Magnon, 4, 14, 37, 73, 91, 94, 113
cultivation, 113
cultural ages, 114

Darwinian evolutionary science, 1, 114
DNA, 114, 130, 131
domestication, 116, 117

Ehringsdorf, 34, 117, 130
epistemology, 117
ethos, 117

finger tracings, 117
flint burins, 117
flint chipping, 118
flint-knapping technique, 118

Galileo, 118
Glaciation, 118, 144, 153

historico-temporal legitimacy, 119
Hominid, 119

Hominidal sequencing, 120
Hominoid, 120
Homo erectus, 6, 34, 38, 39, 105, 120, 126, 136, 147, 156, 157
Homo habilis, 30, 120
Homo hermeneuticus, 7, 30, 56, 72, 83, 120
Homo politicus, 81, 83, 87, 90, 93, 121
Homo Rhodesiensis, 121, 122, 130
Homo sapiens, 11, 30, 33, 34, 36, 37, 38, 39, 40, 56, 58, 72, 74, 94, 95, 109, 113, 115, 118, 119, 120, 121, 122, 126, 129, 130, 131, 134, 135, 138, 145, 152, 154, 157, 160
Homo socialis, 72, 83, 122
Homo soloensis, 27, 39, 122
Homo symbolicum, 7, 122
horticultural wisdom, 123
hunting and gathering, 123
Huxley, Sir Julian, 105, 106, 123, 164, 167

ideology, 41, 124, 163
imagination, 43, 124
interglacial period, 105, 111, 122
interglacial periods, 124

Kant, Emanuel, 45, 50, 124
Kierkegaard, Soren, 44, 125

Levalloisian, 35, 125, 129
ligatures, 125

Magdalenian, 2, 4, 37, 38, 76, 77, 78, 108, 113, 121, 126, 128, 135, 136
malar, 126
masticatory apparatus, 126
maxillary prognathism, 127
memory, 43, 127
Mesolithic Age, 127
microliths, 128
molar dentition, 129
monkeys
  New World, 133
  Old World, 133
Mousterian, 3, 34, 35, 36, 38, 58, 106, 112, 117, 125, 128, 129, 130, 163
myth, 53, 130

Neanderthal, 3, 11, 34, 35, 36, 38, 39, 40, 57, 58, 59, 60, 62, 64, 65, 72, 73, 87, 91, 94, 111, 115, 121, 122, 126, 128, 129, 130, 131, 134, 137, 140, 142, 145, 159, 161, 163, 164
Neolithic Age, 2, 131, 135
Newton, Sir Isaac, 50, 124, 133

occipital aspects, 133
ocher, 133
olfactory sense, 134
olfactory senses, 24, 140, 143

Index   171

oligarchic imperative, 134
opposable digitation, 134

paleodemography, 134
paleographics, 135
Paleolithic Age, 2, 80, 101, 108, 125, 126, 128, 129, 135, 136, 137
percussion technique, 136
Pithecanthropus, 36, 122, 131, 136
Pleistocene, 36, 39, 107, 119, 120, 136, 145, 150, 153, 157
polychrome, 137
polytypic species, 137
portable art, 74, 137
postorbital constriction, 137
power grip, 138
precision grip, 138
prognathesis, 138
propitiate, 138
prosimians, 138, 157
psychodynamic expressiveness, 139
psychogenesis, 29, 139

quadrupedal locomotion, 139

Ramapithecus, 34, 139, 157
reflective self-awareness, 30, 57, 139

reflexive cognition, 31, 139
ritual, 64, 86, 139
Sartre, Jean Paul, 44, 139
savanna, 139
scrimshaw, 140
slash and burn, 140
smell-brain center, 140
sociogenesis, 26, 140
solipsism, 140
Solutrean Culture, 4, 37, 38, 77, 78, 106, 113, 121, 126, 136, 140, 141
Spencer, Herbert, 45, 46, 47, 48, 49, 50, 141, 143
stereoscopic vision, 141
stratiation, 142
supraorbital tori, 142

taurodontism, 142
taxonomy, 142
taxonomy, 149
theologians, 142
transcendental legitimacy, 142
unknowable, 45, 46, 47, 49, 50, 143
unknown, 45, 46, 51, 143
verbal acuity, 143
visual cortex, 143
Wilson, Edward O., 143, 144, 164, 165
worldview, 144
Würm glaciation, 3, 106, 118, 128, 144, 150, 153